THE BROKEN COVENANT

THE
BROKEN
COVENANT

American Civil Religion
in Time of Trial

ROBERT N. BELLAH

A CROSSROAD BOOK The Seabury Press | New York

The Seabury Press
815 Second Avenue
New York, N.Y. 10017

Copyright ©1975 by The Seabury Press, Inc.
Designed by Paula Weiner
Printed in the United States of America

ACKNOWLEDGMENTS

Grateful acknowledgment is extended to the
following publishers for permission to quote from
the copyrighted material listed: The Dial Press for a
selection excerpted from "In Search of a Majority."
Reprinted from the book *Nobody Knows My Name* by
James Baldwin. Copyright © 1954, 1956, 1958,
1959, 1960, 1961 by James Baldwin. Used with
permission of The Dial Press. Grove Press for a
selection from *Tropic of Cancer* by Henry Miller.
Copyright © 1961 by Grove Press, Inc.

LIBRARY OF CONGRESS CATALOGING IN PUBLICATION DATA

Bellah, Robert Neelly, 1927–
    The broken covenant.

    "A Crossroad book."
    "The Weil lectures at Hebrew Union College/Jewish Insti-
tute of Religion in Cincinnati in the fall of 1971."
        1. United States—Civilization—Addresses, essays, lectures.
2. United States—Religion—Addresses, essays, lectures. 3.
United States—Moral conditions—Addresses, essays, lectures. I. Title. II. Series: The Weil lectures, 1971.
E169.1.B435   917.3′03   74–19479
ISBN 0–8164–1161–1

Contents

Preface

T H E six chapters that make up this book were first given as the Weil Lectures at Hebrew Union College/Jewish Institute of Religion in Cincinnati in the fall of 1971, and some of them have been given at other schools since then. In spite of many subsequent revisions the spoken character of the original lectures seemed worth preserving. Since formal speech is perhaps the most native form of conscious American expression, it seemed good that this book retain that traditional characteristic.

From the beginning I would like to acknowledge my amateur status as an Americanist, though not, I hope, as an American. What value the book has lies in its interpretations rather than in new data uncovered. Throughout I have depended on the scholarship of others, most of whom are historians, literary critics, or political scientists, but the primary data are the original texts written or spoken by Americans from the 17th century to the present, that are liberally scattered through every chapter. The purpose of the book is to attempt to understand certain central features of the American tradition from the point of view of the problems of late 20th-century

America. I want to interpret the tradition in terms of the present and the present in terms of the tradition, thus setting up a communication between past and present in the service of enhanced self-understanding.[1] Such an enterprise differs from an effort to explain American society in terms of social and economic variables. It is an exercise in the analysis and interpretation of cultural meaning rather than in sociological explanation, though some of the latter is necessarily present. I view these two types of study as complementary rather than as mutually exclusive.

I grew up in the 1930s and early 1940s in a milieu in which there were few questions about Protestant Christianity or what were taken to be traditional American values. An essentially unbroken affirmation of American society was confirmed in my experience by America's leadership in the great antifascist war. It was not until after my graduation from high school in 1945 that I began to have basic doubts about my society. Thus my experience is fundamentally different from that of those born since the middle forties. I do not think now that the religious and ideological heritage that I was given as a child and as an adolescent was an entirely authentic version of the American tradition, but the subjective sense of continuity with the past is an indelible experience that undoubtedly colors even my present perceptions. My break with American values, when it came, was quite radical, and I went through a period of almost total rejection of my own society.[2] That experience too must influence my present views. But for the last 15 years or so my attitude toward America has embodied a tension—*odi et amo*—of affirmation and rejection. Of all earthly societies I know that this one is mine and I do not regret it. But I also know through objective observation and personal tragedy that this society is a cruel and bitter one, very far, in fact, from its own highest aspirations.

The tension would not be so great for me and, I suspect, for other Americans, if America itself were not built
so centrally on utopian millenial expectations. We shall
be exploring in the course of the book the religious
substructure of these expectations and the distortions
and perversions to which they are subject. But I do not
conclude as some others do that the entire tradition of
religious-moral understanding of America should therefore be abandoned. The substitution, in an effort to de-
mythologize the political system, of a technical-rational
model of politics for a religious-moral one does not seem
to me to be an advantage. Indeed it only exacerbates
tendencies that I think are at the heart of our problems.
If our problems are, as I believe them to be, centrally
moral and even religious, then the effort to sidestep
them with purely technical organizational considerations
can only worsen them. Perhaps a schematic statement of
the argument of the book would be helpful at this point.

It is one of the oldest of sociological generalizations
that any coherent and viable society rests on a common
set of moral understandings about good and bad, right
and wrong, in the realm of individual and social action.
It is almost as widely held that these common moral
understandings must also in turn rest upon a common
set of religious understandings that provide a picture of
the universe in terms of which the moral understandings
make sense. Such moral and religious understandings
produce both a basic cultural legitimation for a society
which is viewed as at least approximately in accord with
them and a standard of judgment for the criticism of a
society that is seen as deviating too far from them. This
conception of the relation between morality, religion,
legitimation, and criticism has not gone unchallenged
either by historic or contemporary writers, but here I can
only assume it and do not defend it. In the 18th century,
as I will attempt to show, there was a common set of

religious and moral understandings rooted in a conception of divine order under a Christian, or at least a deist,
God. The basic moral norms that were seen as deriving
from that divine order were liberty, justice, and charity,
understood in a context of theological and moral discourse which led to a concept of personal virtue as the
essential basis of a good society.

How far we have come from that common set of understandings is illustrated by the almost negative meaning of the word "virtue" today. It is only a step beyond
the derogation of virtue to another current linguistic
usage in which the word "bad" is used to mean "good."
It is not my point that people in the 18th century were
more virtuous or better than people today. The relation
between language, morality, and behavior is not so simple. The erosion of language, however, is a symptom of
the erosion of common meanings, of which there is a
great deal of evidence in our society. This takes the form,
which is by now statistically well documented, of a decline of belief in all forms of obligation: to one's occupation, one's family, and one's country. A tendency to rank
personal gratification above obligation to others corre-
lates with a deepening cynicism about the established
social, economic, and political institutions of society. A
sense that the basic institutions of society are unjust and
serve the interests of a few at the expense of the many,
is used to justify the inapplicability of moral obligations
to one's self.

For some this disillusion with the moral validity of
American institutions leads to a passionate sense of injustice and a struggle for a more just society. But for
many others it leads only to an admiration of the few who
have manipulated the system in their own favor, and to
a desire to emulate them, if not in actuality, then in
fantasy. Nor would it be difficult to show that the main-

line churches, Protestant and Catholic, that have provided the religious framework for the traditional morality, are in disarray, have declining income and attendance, and themselves are the objects of the same suspicion with which all established institutions are viewed. There are very important countertendencies to this moral and religious erosion in particular sectors of the society that will be investigated later, tendencies both to conserve the old understandings and to pioneer radically new ones. But the major tendency in the society at large seems to be erosion rather than reaction or reconstruction.

The erosion of common moral and religious understandings is not identical with increasing moral and social corruption, though there is much evidence of the latter in contemporary America. The increase of crimes against persons and property has many causes, and a declining sense of the immorality of such crimes is certainly one of them. The increase of shoplifting by people of all social classes is a case in point, especially when the excuse, from youths who are by no means radical activists, is that one is "only ripping off the capitalists." Far more serious is the corrosion of morality at the highest reaches of government and business of which we have heard so much in recent times. In spite of the widespread outcries, it remains to be seen whether the internalized moral restraints among the powerful have really been strengthened.

Yet simultaneous with widespread evidence of corruption has been continuous pressure for higher standards of moral behavior. Eighteenth-century Americans with a few notable exceptions tolerated slavery; we do not. Nineteenth-century Americans tolerated violence and discrimination against immigrants and ethnic minorities; we do not. The early 20th century tolerated the notion that women were basically inferior to men, even while giving them the vote; we do not. In the treatment of blacks, ethnic minorities, and women we still have far to go, but it would be hard to argue that we were better in these respects at any earlier period in our history.

The paradox of a declining sense of moral obligation, together with a heightened sense of distributive justice, may be partially explained by observing that both phenomena reflect the influence of the last remaining element of the common value system: individual freedom. In the 17th and 18th centuries, as we will see, freedom was part of a whole articulated framework of moral and religious values—it meant freedom to do the good and was almost equivalent to virtue. Under the rising criticism of utilitarianism, first in the late 18th century and then with ever greater insistence in the 19th and 20th centuries, freedom came to mean freedom to pursue self-interest, latterly defined as "freedom to do your own thing." To the extent that the Puritan and early republican notions of "the good" and "virtue" were too narrow, too bound up with repressive social and psychological mechanisms, too easily subverted to the defense of particular social arrangements, the utilitarian critique has been genuinely liberating. To the extent that the utilitarian critique was not itself able to construct a moral-religious context for a viable society, it has had to fall back on an uneasy symbiosis with the traditional pattern that it continues to undermine. As the older moral pattern declines in persuasiveness, the only remaining category for the analysis and evaluation of human motives is interest, which by now has replaced both virtue and conscience in our moral vocabulary.

Interest is itself a valid concern and the term has of course been part of the traditional systems of moral thought, but the common-sense utilitarianism that has become the dominant mode of American public morality has torn interest from its larger traditional context and understands it only in terms of the self-interest of the isolated individual. Whether the notion of self, lacking any larger identifications with social and religious realities, and the notion of interest without any encompassing context of loyalties and obligations, can provide a coherent morality for a viable society is certainly open to doubt. The present state of American society is not encouraging with respect to the outcome of that experiment. And we must remember that, no matter how undermined, a remnant of the older morality provides much of what coherence our society still has.

The utilitarian morality of self-interest is only one element of a much larger social and cultural complex that has become increasingly dominant in the last two or three centuries. The rise of science on the one hand and of a market economy and industrial capitalism on the other have been important elements in that complex. The rise of commercial and then industrial capitalism in America neither explains everything nor dictates everything, but it can hardly be ignored. The affinity between this mode of economic organization and certain modes of moral and cognitive culture that have roots deep in western culture undoubtedly helps explain why those modes, utilitarianism and science, have become such central cultural forms in modern America. The complex of capitalism, utilitarianism, and science as a cultural form has its own world view, its own "religion" even— though it is an adamantly this-worldly one—and its own utopianism: the utopianism of total technical control, of course in the service of the "freedom" of individual self-interest. The political expression of this complex is a technical-regulative conception of political society in which the state is seen as an essentially neutral arbiter among the contending interest groups, whose competition and countervailing pressures are assumed to guarantee the interest of all.

Much criticism of American society has been based on the acceptance of the rational, technical, utilitarian ideology that I have briefly outlined, and it has been concerned to point out the extent to which that model does not in fact operate very well: that the state is not neutral as between interest groups; the self-interest of some Americans is much better served than the self-interest of others, and so forth. The critical intent of this book is quite different. I hope to show that the liberal utilitarian model was not the fundamental religious and moral conception of America, open as the latter was in certain directions to the development of that model. That original conception, which has never ceased to be operative, was based on an imaginative religious and moral conception of life that took account of a much broader range of social, ethical, aesthetic, and religious needs than the utilitarian model can deal with. Without arguing for the literal revival of that earlier conception, I hope to show that only a new imaginative, religious, moral, and social context for science and technology will make it possible to weather the storms that seem to be closing in on us in the late 20th century. I am convinced that the continued and increased dominance of the complex of capitalism, utilitarianism, and the belief that the only road to truth is science will rapidly lead to the destruction of American society, or possibly in an effort to stave off destruction, to a technical tyranny of the "brave new world" variety.

Still I do not want to present a simple scenario of good guys and bad guys. I do not think that the theologians and poets in America have all been saints and the industrialists and technicians all devils. Our technical rational accomplishments have been stunning, and if they could ever be brought into a context of genuine human sympathy, they could greatly relieve suffering both in America and all over the world. I cannot exonerate the tradition of religious and moral self-understanding, which I am trying to understand and in part reappropriate, from a share of responsibility in our present trials. The Pilgrim Fathers had a conception of the covenant and of virtue which we badly need today. But almost from the moment they touched American soil they broke that covenant and engaged in unvirtuous actions.

The story of America is a somber one, filled with great achievements and great crimes. Ours is a society that has amassed more wealth and power than any other in history. I am not sure that Americans or any other group of human beings have yet attained the wisdom to use such power without self-destruction. I am convinced, though, that the first step toward that wisdom is humility in the face of who we are and where we have come from. If this book makes even a small contribution toward that humility it will not have been in vain.

When I was an undergraduate at Harvard I attended the lectures of F.O. Matthiessen, one of the greatest Americanists of the century. His book, *The American Rennaissance,* is the wisest of all the books about America that I have read. In addition to being a great scholar Matthiessen embodied the tragic dimension of American culture in his own life. It is to his memory that this book is dedicated.

My indebtednesses are many. In particular I would like to thank Professor Samuel Sandmel, chairman of the Frank L. Weil Foundation, for his hospitality during my time at the Hebrew Union College/Jewish Institute of Religion. Dr. Sandmel and his wife and others associated with the Institute made my stay in Cincinnati a pleasant one. Conrad Cherry and Eli Sagan gave the manuscript a careful reading and made many helpful suggestions. Mrs. Julia Cleland helped with the manuscript and in this as in other projects gave her unfailing support and assistance.

Berkeley, California
June, 1974

I

America's Myth of Origin

ONCE in each of the last three centuries America has faced a time of trial, a time of testing so severe that not only the form but even the existence of our nation have been called in question. Born out of the revolutionary crisis of the Atlantic world in the late 18th century, America's first time of trial was our struggle for independence and the institution of liberty. The second time of trial came not long before the end of the nation's first hundred years. At stake was the preservation of the union and the extension of equal protection of the laws to all members of society. We live at present in a third time of trial at least as severe as those of the Revolution and the Civil War. It is a test of whether our inherited institutions can be creatively adapted to meet the 20th-century crisis of justice and order at home and in the world. It is a test of whether republican liberty established in a remote agrarian backwater of the world in the 18th century shall prove able or willing to confront successfully the age of mass society and international revolution. It is a test of whether we can control the very economic and technical forces, which are our greatest achievement, before they destroy us.

In the beginning, and to some extent ever since, Americans have interpreted their history as having religious meaning. They saw themselves as being a "people" in the classical and biblical sense of the word. They hoped they were a people of God. They often found themselves to be a people of the devil. American history, like the history of any people, has within it archetypal patterns that reflect the general condition of human beings as pilgrims and wanderers on this earth. Founded in an experience of transcendent order, the new settlements habitually slipped away from their high calling and fell into idolatry, as the children of Israel had done before them. Time and again there have arisen prophets to recall this people to its original task, its errand into the wilderness. Significant accomplishments in building a just society have alternated with corruption and despair in America, as in other lands, because the struggle to institutionalize humane values is endless on this earth. But at times the issue grows acute. A period of history hangs in the balance. A people finds that it must decide whether its immediate future will be better or worse, and sometimes whether it will have a future at all.

I wish to examine the history of America's religious self-understanding, the myths that have developed to help us interpret who and what we are in America and to inquire whether they may still have power to help us understand our present situation and know how to deal with it. The present situation has, therefore, influenced the selection I have made from the materials of the past. It has not, I hope, dictated the outcome of my inquiry. We need truth whether it is comforting or whether it is dismaying. While committed to the pursuit of how it has actually been in America, I am not uninvolved in the outcome. I am convinced that in these last years of the 20th century the republic is in danger. If we believe that it is worth saving, then we must know what it is that we wish to save, not holding with a deathly grip to an unchanging past but seeking the inspiration to undertake that reformation, reconstruction, and reconstitution which are necessary.

This book is not primarily about political theory or about ideology, though both are involved, but about religion and myth. In particular I will be reexamining the American civil religion[1] and the mythological structure that supports it. By civil religion I refer to that religious dimension, found I think in the life of every people, through which it interprets its historical experience in the light of transcendent reality. I do not want, at this point, to argue abstractly the validity of the concept "civil religion." I hope to demonstrate its usefulness. In using the word "myth," I do not mean to suggest a story that is not true. Myth does not attempt to describe reality; that is the job of science. Myth seeks rather to transfigure reality so that it provides moral and spiritual meaning to individuals or societies. Myths, like scientific theories, may be true or false, but the test of truth or falsehood is different.

2

America's myth of origin is a strategic point of departure because the comparative study of religion has found that where a people conceives itself to have started reveals much about its most basic self-conceptions. At first glance the problem of origin in America seems a relatively simple one. Unlike most historic peoples, America as a nation began on a definite date, July Fourth, 1776. Thus, in analyzing America's myth of origin, close attention must be paid to the mythic significance of the Declaration of Independence, which is considerable. Or taking a less precise definition of beginning, one might consider the whole period, from the Declaration of Independence to the inauguration of Washington under the new Constitution, as the origin time of the American nation. America began as the result of a series of conscious decisions. The acts embodying those decisions have a kind of absolute meaning-creating significance. As Hannah Arendt says, "What saves the act of beginning from its own arbitrariness is that it carries its own principle within itself, or, to be more precise, that beginning and principle, *principium* and principle, are not only related to each other, but are coeval."[2] We will want to consider the act of conscious meaning-creation, or conscious taking responsibility for oneself and one's society, as a central aspect of America's myth of origin, an act that, by the very radicalness of its beginning, a beginning *ex nihilo* as it were, is redolent of the sacred. The sacredness of the Constitution, which is closely bound up with the existence of the American people, derives largely from that source since it does not, not explicitly at least (and in this it differs from the Declaration of Independence), call upon any source of sacredness higher than itself and its makers.[3]

And yet those datable acts of beginning, radical though they were, and archetypal for all later reflection about America, were themselves mythic gestures which could not but stir up, at the beginning and later, the images and symbols of earlier myths and mythically interpreted histories. In human affairs no beginning is absolutely new and every beginning takes meaning from some counterpoint of similarity to and difference from earlier events. Indeed when we look closely at the beginning time of the American republic we find not a simple unitary myth of origin but a complex and richly textured mythical structure with many inner tensions. One way to begin is to consider the profoundly mythic meaning of

"America" long before the founding of the United States, a meaning that was by no means obliterated but in some ways reinforced by the establishment of the new nation.

3

The origin myth of America in this broader perspective is origin itself. According to John Locke, "In the beginning all the world was America."[4] America stood for the primordial state of the world and man and was indeed seen, by the first generations of Europeans to learn of it, to be the last remaining remnant of that earlier time. The newness which was so prominent an attribute of what was called the "new" world was taken not just as newness to its European discoverers and explorers but as newness in some pristine and absolute sense: newness from the hands of God. That sense of indelible newness, which has been a blessing and a curse throughout our history, has not evaporated even today. If it gives us a sense that we come from nowhere, that our past is inchoate and our tradition shallow, so that we begin to doubt our own identity and some of the sensitive among us flee to more ancient lands with more structured traditions, it also gives us our openness to the future, our sense of unbounded possibility, our willingness to start again in a new place, a new occupation, a new ideology. Santayana has spoken of "the moral emptiness of a settlement where men and even houses are easily moved about, and no one, almost, lives where he was born or believes what he has been taught."[5] Yet other Europeans have envied our capacity to act without being immobilized by ancient institutions.

The newness of America, so prominent in the consciousness of the early European observers, and which we have still not entirely outgrown even though it is nearly 500 years since Columbus (from the point of view of Europe) "discovered" America, had another important consequence. For the early explorers, and certainly for those in Europe reading their first reports, the specificity and detail of America's native flora and fauna, and even more, its aboriginal Indian cultures, which by 1492 had already completed a long and distinguished history in this hemisphere, were swallowed up in a generalized feeling of newness which replaced that specificity and detail with the blank screen of an alleged "state of nature." Upon that screen they projected certain fantasies, dreams, and nightmares long carried in the baggage of European tradition but seldom heretofore finding so vivid and concrete an objective correlative. Thus America came to be thought of as a paradise and a wilderness, with all of the rich associations of those terms in the Christian and biblical traditions, or, more simply, thus Europeans came to think of America as both a heaven and a hell.

4

Locke, who, as we have seen, tended to identify America with the state of nature, defined the latter as "a State of Peace, Goodwill, Mutual Assistance, and Preservation." And he goes on to say, "Men living together according to reason, without a common Superior on Earth, with Authority to judge between them, is *properly the State of Nature.*"[6] This description conforms admirably with Columbus's description of life in his newly discovered West Indies:

The people of this island, and of all the other islands which I have found and of which I have information, all go naked, men and women, as their mothers bore them, although some women cover a single place with the leaf of a plant or with a net of cotton which they make for the purpose. They have no iron or steel or weapons, nor are they fitted to use them, not because they are not well built and of handsome stature, but because they are very marvellously timorous. They have no other arms than weapons made of canes, cut in seeding time, to the ends of which they fix a small sharpened stick. . . . they are so guileless and so generous with all they possess, that no one would believe it who has not seen it. They never refuse anything which they possess, if it be asked of them; on the contrary, they invite anyone to share it, and display so much love as if they would give their hearts. . . . And they do not know any creed and are not idolators; only they all believe that power and good are in the heavens . . . not . . . because they are ignorant; on the contrary, they are of a very acute intelligence and are men who navigate all these seas.[7]

His description suggests the paradisic imagery which clearly lies just below the surface of this and many other early descriptions of the American Indians, descriptions that quickly catapulted them into the central representatives of Adamic man in the European imagination. The emphasis is, above all, on innocence as expressed in the Indians' nakedness, so striking to the heavily clad Europeans; their freedom about sexual relations; their lack of any discernible government; their communal sharing of property; and their lack of either religious dogmas or priests. And to complete the Edenic picture was their total lack of aggression. Why indeed should anyone be aggressive in a land where fruit was to be had for the picking, game for the trapping, and all good things were abundantly at hand, even including gold?

Even when experience began to render a rather different picture of the land and its people, the search for a literal Eden went on, especially in Latin America. Already Columbus believed he had located the general site where the earthly paradise would be found and imagined that fresh-water currents in the sea off the northern coast of South America actually flowed from it.[8] With literal-minded doggedness others would seek El Dorado, the Seven Cities of Cibola, or the Fountain of Eternal Youth. While the paradisic expectations of the English colonists were not so fully developed as those further South they were strong enough to cause early Maryland to be described as an "Earthly Paradise" and Georgia as "that promis'd Canaan."[9] The Sicilian immigrants who arrived in New York expecting the streets to be paved with gold, or the little old ladies who invest their life savings in California land developers' schemes to "make the desert blossom like the rose" are only late incarnations of an old dream about the New World.

5

But there was another picture of America, closer to Hobbes than to Locke, that is also present from the beginning. Unlike the paradisic view, it dwelt on scorching deserts and uncrossable mountains, hurricanes and floods, tropical heat and arctic cold. In accordance with this violent and extreme landscape, the second view found the native inhabitants anything but innocent. Instead they were depicted as "horrid savages" devoted to murder, rape, human sacrifice, and cannibalism and prepared to use every ruse of cunning and treachery. Led by cruel and despotic chieftains the Indians were described as spending the time left over from murder, plunder, and rapine in the barbaric worship of a vast array of demons, chief of whom was the devil himself. The Hobbesian image of the American state of nature was not paradise but wilderness, in the most negative sense of that word: unfruitful desert, abode of death.

America was, when first discovered, and to some extent even today, a vast unknown to the Europeans who explored and settled it. It is not surprising that anything so vast, so significant, and so little known as the new world would arouse in those who contemplated it the deepest wishes and the darkest fears. The paradise theme has been more prominent and more conscious, but those who believe that the American dream, the paradisic hope, has but lately turned into a nightmare, suffer from illusion. The nightmare was there from the beginning. There is, of course, an inner affinity between dream and nightmare. It is an old story in history that a dream of paradise can motivate hellish actions, and each new-world El Dorado was won at the expense of nightmarish enslavement or extermination of Indians and often unspeakable internecine brutalities among Europeans.

For all the new European inhabitants of America the Christian and biblical tradition provided images and symbols with which to interpret the enormous hopes and fears aroused in them by their new situation, as I have already suggested in using the terms "paradise" and "wilderness." The English colonists, especially in New England, had a particular version of that interpretation, one that contained a dialectical relationship between wilderness and paradise. That dialectic must be seen against the background of a vast mythic scenario which began to unfold in Europe—providentially, the Puritan fathers thought—just after the discovery of the New World. That scenario was the Protestant Reformation, and it was an informing event in the background not only of the Puritans in New England but of most of the settlers in the middle and southern colonies as well.

6

The idea of reform[10] is far older than the Reformation and is, in fact, central to Christianity itself. It is related to the idea of conversion, the turning from evil to good, from self to God, which is close to the heart of the biblical message in both testaments. Reformation is a kind of renovation or renewal, making new, particularly stressed in the letters of Paul. In II Corinthians 5:17 Paul writes, "If then any be in Christ a new creature, the old things are passed away, behold, all things are made new." The primary reference of the concept of reformation or renewal is the soul of the individual. Renewal is embodied in the sacramental life of the church in the sacrament of baptism, a kind of rebirth which brings the individual into the church, the communion of saints, who, because they are in Christ, share a provisional form of paradise. But the church itself may need renewal, and thus another meaning for the term developed. Monasticism was a kind of reform and could lead to movements of reform more generally in the church, as with Augustine, Benedict, or Bernard of Clairvaux.

Finally, always in the background and occassionally in the foreground, was the notion that the world itself is in need of reform and rebirth. The last book of the New Testament, Revelation, was the bearer of such ideas of millennial renewal, of an age of holiness when Christ would return and rule on earth, ideas that time and again broke out into movements of millennial expectation. The Reformation was a heightening and intensification of all these ideas. It began above all as a reform of the church, but it led to a more rigorous stress on the reform of the individual soul, particularly the lay soul, than had been common in the medieval church, and it also carried overtones of apocalyptic expectation. The Roman Church was identified with the Whore of Babylon and the Protestant Church with the New Jerusalem as they are described in Revelation. In this perspective the Reformation could be interpreted as an event presaging the end of times and the birth of a new heaven and a new earth.

The symbolic connections between the heightened consciousness of renewal and rebirth brought on by the Reformation and the discovery and settlement of a "new" world are obvious enough, but the connections are greatly intensified when we consider how closely the notion of "wilderness" in the Bible is tied in with the renewal theme. Christ's forty days in the wilderness following his baptism by John the Baptist were often interpreted as symbolic of purification and renewal before beginning his ministry, and the monks who withdrew to the desert were in a sense following his example. Following the method of typological interpretation,[11] which saw Old Testament events as prefiguring New Testament ones, the 40 years that the children of Israel spent wandering in the wilderness of Sinai were interpreted as a figure of Christ's 40 days. The Israelites were being tested, purified, and renewed for entering into their inheritance of the Promised Land, as Christ was being prepared for his inheritance at the right hand of the Father.

The wilderness theme was also linked to the millenial imagery in an important passage of Revelation 12:6: "and the woman fled into the wilderness, where she had a place prepared by God, in which to be nourished for one thousand two hundred and sixty days." The "woman" was interpreted to be God's true Church which would have to flee to a prepared place in the wilderness just before the end of times.

Now all of these references and quite a few more, including some in the Song of Songs and in several of the postexilic prophets, were used by the New England fathers to interpret their situation. They saw themselves on a divinely appointed "errand into the wilderness" with profound personal, ecclesiastical, and world-historical meaning. Under the circumstances, wilderness was by no means entirely a negative concept. It was a place of danger and temptation, but the "enclosed garden" that the saints were required to build up in the midst of the wilderness was itself a foretaste of paradise.[12] And as Jonathan Edwards and others came to believe, it was precisely here, in the wilderness of the new world, that God was most likely to begin his new heaven and new earth. A precarious but fruitful balance between hope and fear had been struck.

7

The Bible was the one book that literate Americans in the 17th, 18th, and 19th centuries could be expected to know well. Biblical imagery provided the basic framework for imaginative thought in America up until quite recent times and, unconsciously, its control is still formidable. The typological or figural interpretation of the Puritans is neither higher biblical criticism nor scientific history. Both of these more recent endeavors have their uses but the mythical level of human consciousness cannot be satisfied by them. A tradition of living myth is always typological in this sense: it sees connections and analogies between many different elements in the tradition and it interprets current events and predicaments in terms of traditional motifs. When Protestant literalism and enlightenment rationalism became dominant in the late 18th and 19th centuries, typological interpretation was taken up covertly by the novelists and poets or began to operate at unconscious or semiconscious levels of popular culture and ideology. The split between rational and mythic discourse which has characterized our recent cultural history is very dangerous for it impoverishes both modes of thought.[13] It is one of the possible benefits of the current new appreciation of the meaning and function of myth that we may be able to rescue it from the realm of unconscious fantasy where it always continues to operate, often in dark and devious ways, and restore it once again to its creative role in human consciousness. At any rate it is my purpose to suggest some of the ways in which biblical (and other) imagery has operated powerfully, consciously and unconsciously, to shape the American interpretation of reality and to some extent the actions of Americans in the world.

8

In our search for America's myth of origin we have considered the function the new continent served in the European consciousness and the way in which biblical themes, particularly as heightened by the Reformation, shaped its meaning. We have set the scene and brought in the stage furniture but we have not begun the drama. A myth of origin for America must point to certain events in America, not only to their archetypal foreshadowings in biblical history.

Fortunately we have a document from the earliest period in American history which expresses beautifully the various ideas we have been assembling. The document is a sermon preached by John Winthrop, the first leader of the Massachusetts Bay Colony, on board ship in 1630 even before landing in the new world. It defines the meaning of the new venture and its implications and obligations for the new settlers. Of it Perry Miller has written, ". . . in relation to the principal theme of the American mind, the necessity laid upon it for decision, Winthrop stands at the beginning of our consciousness."[14] The sermon is called "A Modell of Christian Charity."

Thus stands the cause betweene God and us. Wee are entered into Covenant with him for this worke, wee have taken
out a Commission, the Lord hath given us leave to draw our
owne Articles, wee have professed to enterprise these Accions
upon these and these ends, wee have hereupon besought him
of favour and blessing: Now if the Lord shall please to heare
us, and bring us in peace to the place wee desire, then hath hee
ratified this Covenant and sealed our Commission [and] will
expect a strickt performance of the Articles contained in it, but
if wee shall neglect the observacion of these Articles which are
the ends wee have propounded, and dissembling with our
God, shall fall to embrace this present world and prosecute
our carnall intencions seekeing great things for our selves
and our posterity, the Lord will surely breake out in wrathe
against us, be revenged of such a perjured people and make
us knowe the price of the breache of such a Covenant.

Now the onely way to avoyde this shipwracke and to provide
for our posterity is to followe the Counsell of Micah, to doe
Justly, to love mercy, to walke humbly with our God. For this
end, wee must be knitt together in this worke as one man, wee
must entertaine each other in brotherly Affeccion, wee must be
willing to abridge our selves of our superfluities, for the supply
of others necessities, wee must uphold a familiar Commerce
together in all meeknes, gentlenes, patience and liberallity,
wee must delight in each other, make others Condicions our
owne, rejoyce together, mourne together, labour and suffer
together, allwayes haveing before our eyes our Commission
and Community in the worke, our Community as members of
the same body, soe shall wee keepe the unitie of the spirit in
the bond of peace, the Lord will be our God and delight to
dwell among us as his owne people and will commaund a
blessing upon us in all our wayes, soe that wee shall see much
more of his wisdome, power, goodnes and truthe than formerly wee have beene acquainted with. Wee shall finde that
the God of Israell is among us, when tenn of us shall be able
to resist a thousand of our enemies, when hee shall make us
a prayse and glory, that men shall say of succeeding planta-

cions: the lord make it like that of New England: for wee must
Consider that wee shall be as a Citty upon a Hill, the eies of
all people are uppon us: soe that if wee shall deale falsely with
our god in this worke wee have undertaken and soe cause him
to withdrawe his present help from us, wee shall shame the
faces of many of gods worthy servants, and cause theire pray-
ers to be turned into Cursses upon us till wee be consumed out
of the good land whither wee are goeing: And to shutt upp this
discourse with that exhortacion of Moses, that faithfull servant
of the Lord in his last farewell to Isreall, Deut. 30. Beloved
there is now sett before us life, and good, deathe and evill in
that wee are Commaunded this day to love the Lord our God,
and to love one another, to walke in his wayes and to keepe
his Commaundements and his Ordinance, and his lawes, and
the Articles of our Covenant with him that wee may live and
be multiplied, and that the Lord our God may blesse us in the
land whither we goe to possesse it: But if our heartes shall
turne away soe that wee will not obey, but shall be seduced and
worship . . . other Gods, our pleasures, and proffitts, and serve
them; it is propounded unto us this day, wee shall surely
perishe out of the good Land whither wee passe over this vast
Sea to possesse it;

> Therefore lett us choose life,
> that wee, and our Seede,
> may live; by obeyeing his
> voyce, and cleaveing to him,
> for hee is our life, and
> our prosperity.[15]

The Deuteronomic formula of the blessing and the
curse is John Winthrop's way of summing up the meaning of the immense hopes and fears of the colonists in
the face of the unknown land that lay ahead. He turned
the ocean-crossing into a crossing of the Red Sea and the
Jordan River and he held out the hope that Massachusetts Bay would be a promised land. Most of the colonists
were men and women who had been profoundly con-

verted, inwardly reformed and renewed, and who felt uneasy and unhappy about continuing to live in an England where they felt much was corrupt in church and state. But even before they had freed themselves from the bonds of English society they had undertaken an "Agreement" in Cambridge, England, the year before and bound themselves to a new covenant with obligations both to God and one another.[16] The "Agreement" of the Massachusetts Bay Colony was a beginning that contained its own principle, just as, as we have seen, the acts establishing the new republic did. But here the archetypes that the mythic gestures of beginning point to are much more explicit. Here too is one of those mythic precursors to which, explicitly or not, the act of the founding of the republic itself inevitably pointed.

9

In his contrast between charity and the worship of pleasure and profit Winthrop echoes Augustine's great contrast of *caritas* as the principle of the City of God and *cupiditas* as the principle of the earthly city.[17] Augustine in turn was elaborating the New Testament contrast between Babylon, the city of the beast, the principalities and powers of this world, and the New Jerusalem, the Heavenly City where the saints would be gathered after the apocalypse. Of course neither in the New Testament nor in Augustine did the New Jerusalem appear as a political community in this world. For Augustine even the church was but a foreshadowing of the Heavenly City which remains invisible on this earth, since the visible church contains many who will in the end turn out not to be citizens of the Heavenly City. Political society he saw largely in negative terms, at best a punishment and correction of sin, at worst a nightmare of corruption in which the strong eat up the weak and the stronger eat up the strong. Although the Augustinian note is evident in Winthrop and the New England Puritans, and although Winthrop also saw the new colony not as the New Jerusalem itself, which would be brought about only by God's direct intervention, but only as a foretaste of it, Winthrop was fundamentally more positive toward the political order than Augustine had been. Winthrop was, unlike Augustine, the leader of a total society in which church and state, though different, were closely connected and in which Christianity informed the political as well as the religious structure.

John Calvin, the great European predecessor of the New England Puritans, working carefully from a basically Augustinian starting point, had argued that a well-ordered nonmonarchical church could operate symbiotically with a well-ordered polity, namely the city-republic of Geneva, to create an ethical social order. He had managed to restore much of the dignity of the classical conception of political order and to combine Christian charity with civic virtue. The Calvinist Christian commonwealth would not be the City of God on earth but it could be a worthy harbinger of it. It was this conception that the New England Puritans brought to America where it was enhanced by the millenial expectations of which we have spoken.

There was, then, a strongly social, communal, or collective emphasis in early New England political thought. That collective emphasis, that understanding of man as fundamentally social, was derived from the classical conception of the *polis* as responsible for the education and the virtue of its citizens, from the Old Testament notion of the Covenant between God and a people held collectively responsible for its actions, and from the New Testament notion of a community based on charity or love and expressed in brotherly affection and fellow membership in one common body. This collective emphasis did not mean a denigration of the individual because the Calvinist synthesis of the older traditions maintained a strong sense of the dignity and responsibility of the individual and especially stressed voluntaristic individual action. But Calvinist "individualism" only made sense within the collective context. Individual action outside the bounds of religious and moral norms was seen in Augustinian terms as the very archetype of sin.

10

This dual emphasis on the individual and on society can be traced in the dialectic of conversion and covenant that was continuously worked over in the colonial Protestant Churches and came to provide a series of feelings, images, and concepts that would help shape the meaning of the new republic. To the early Puritans, conversion was an intensely personal and individual experience of salvation, and the prerequisite of church membership. A public account of such a personal experience, subject to inquiry and examination and the confirmation of goodly moral character, was required from each prospective member. While the Puritans were aware that members of the church, conceived as the Covenant of Grace, were ultimately known only to God and that it was almost certain that there were hypocrites in the visible church, they tried as far as possible to maintain a church of the converted. In addition to the inward covenant there was also the outward or national covenant to which all New Englanders were conceived of as belonging or at least to which they were subject. This was the basis of civil society. Ideally, individual conversion and external covenant should go together and there were those who tried to blur the distinction in practice as well, but there was also a long tradition of concern over the tension that usually exists between the two.

Conversion, following traditions deeply rooted in both testaments of the Bible, was felt to be a form of liberation. To be converted was to be freed from the bondage of sin and death, emancipated from slavery to the world, the flesh, and the devil. The Reformation emphasized that the converted man is a free man, in certain respects answerable only to God. Evangelical preachers in the 18th century often expatiated on the theme of the "sweets of liberty."[18] But conversion as a liberating experience was always balanced by the coordinate concept of covenant, which implied a definite set of obligations between God and man and between man and man. Much of the controversy of colonial piety emerged from the effort to keep a balance between conversion and covenant. The long struggle over whether a conversion experience was essential for church membership was an argument over whether the unconverted could share in the covenant relation with the converted and attain at least some of the worldly and spiritual advantages of church membership. The Great Awakening, the wave of religious revivals that swept through all the colonies in the 1740s, aroused the passionate involvement of Jonathan Edwards and others who shared his opposition to a church based on the external covenant alone. They hoped the Awakening would serve as a channel of grace through which most or all of the community could be converted and thus share fully in the obligations and rewards of the covenant.

But the Awakening raised the specter of unbalance in the other direction. Some of those carried away by the emotional enthusiasm of the revival interpreted their new spiritual liberation as freedom from any law whatsoever. Others, less obvious than the open antinomians, interpreted their inner emotional experiences as guarantees of their salvation without any further need for action in the world. Edwards, in his *Treatise Concerning Religious*

Affections,[19] is at pains to counter both of these errors. He developed a scheme of 12 signs indicative of the genuineness of the conversion experience. Among the most important of them were: a genuine and permanent transformation in the nature of the convert, that is of his whole personality in relation to his environment; and the last and most fully described sign, the actual practice, both religious and ethical, which the genuine convert would show in his subsequent life. The strong note of social responsibility struck in Winthrop's conception of the covenant continued in the line of Calvinist and evangelical thought in the 18th century. Conversion was not just an act of purely private piety. The liberty flowing from it did not mean escape from social obligations. Covenant liberty was seen as profoundly social as in the following quotation from the leading 18th-century Baptist Isaac Backus:

The true liberty of man is, to know, obey and enjoy his Creator, and to do all the good unto, and enjoy all the happiness with and in his fellow creatures that he is capable of; in order to which the law of love was written in his heart, which carries in it's nature union and benevolence to Being in general, and to each being in particular, according to it's nature and excellency, and to it's relation and connexion with the supreme Being, and ourselves. Each rational soul, as he is part of the whole system of rational beings, so it was and is, both his duty and his liberty, to regard the good of the whole in all his actions.[20]

The juncture of liberty and duty in Backus's last sentence is the key to the Protestant conception of liberty in relation to conversion and covenant. Opposed to external compulsion in religion and, as the decades passed, ever more explicitly in politics as well, they retained a profound sense of obligation both to higher law and to "the good of the whole." Edwards noted with disapproval the common "notion of liberty" as "a person's having the opportunity of doing as he pleases." And Isaac Backus noted that all government "in the imagination of many, interferes with such liberty."[21] But if the evangelical leaders recoiled from antinomianism and anarchy, they recoiled equally from a cold "external covenant." Genuine covenant obligations to God and other men were to be joyfully accepted in the warm hearts of the converted. The restraint of a purely exterior law involving no inner assent was to them not much better than no law at all. And indeed they stood ready to exhort their fellows to throw off such involuntary external constraint when the hour came to do so.

11

So far we have confined our investigation to biblical events and images, elaborated in the colonial experience, and how they came to provide a structure of mythic meaning for the great founding events of the republic. But the Bible was not the only source of myth and symbol for the new nation.

The English political tradition was the major influence on colonial thought and institutions, and references to it were copious. In the mounting controversy that preceded the Revolution references to the British Constitution and "the rights of Englishmen" were innumerable. In many respects the unprecedented degree of self-government existing in the colonies almost from the beginning was due to specifically English political and constitutional developments and would not have been tolerated by any other major colonial power. And yet there is remarkably little to show of English influence in the new republic at the level of myth and symbol. Even granted that this is mainly due to hostility toward Britain generated by the Revolution itself ("The British," said Jefferson, "are in our bowels and we must expel them."),[22] it might well have been possible to turn to some earlier period in English history—Magna Carta, say, or the Protectorate under Cromwell—to provide a body of legitimating symbols for the new nation. But the only major body of nonbiblical symbols that we find in the words and acts of the founding fathers is not English but Roman.

For several centuries before the American Revolution the history of the Roman republic had figured prominently in the imagination of educated Europe. Modern political theory from Machiavelli to Montesquieu had been preoccupied with understanding its greatness and its decline. Latin literature was at the core of humanistic education in America as well as Europe. Virgil's Aeneid even fitfully rivalled the Exodus of the Children of Israel as an archetypal story of flight into the wilderness in order to found a new city. Just as Winthrop thought of Moses so Captain John Smith thought of Aeneas in what Howard Mumford Jones calls the "prose Aeneid" that he composed to recount his establishment of the English Colony in Virginia.[23] But it was not so much Latin myth or legend that dominated the minds of educated Americans in the late 18th century as it was the history of Roman liberty. It was this history which served as both archetype and warning. As Joseph Warren wrote in 1772 in commemorating the second anniversary of the Boston massacre: "It was *this* noble attachment to a free constitution, which raised ancient Rome from the smallest beginnings to that bright summit of happiness and glory to which she arrived; and it was the loss of *this* which plunged her from *that* summit into the black gulph of infamy and slavery."[24]

It is not surprising then that Roman classicism dominated the surface symbolism of the new republic. Its very
terminology was latinate, the words "republic," "president," "congress," and "senate," being Latin in origin
and clearly distinct from the terminology for their British
counterparts. The great seal of the United States bears
two Latin mottos, *E pluribus unum* and *Novus ordo saeclorum*
(new order of the ages), though even the Virgilian reference of the latter should not blind us to the biblical level
of meaning that it also carries. George Washington, the
Cincinnatus of the West, went to his inauguration by
passing under arches of laurel. Greco-Roman classicism
dominated the architecture and much of the art of the
early republican period.[25]

At a deeper level, the Roman attribute that preoccupied the imagination of the founders of the new nation
was republican virtue, especially as it was interpreted by
Montesquieu, the great forerunner of modern sociology
and one of the political thinkers most influential on late
18th century America. According to Montesquieu, in his
tripartite scheme of despotism, monarchy, and republic,
each type of society has its own principle of social life
which provides the spring of action for its members. For
despotism that principle is fear. For monarchy it is
honor: the spirit of emulation, what today we might call
status seeking. For a republic, and especially for its democratic rather than aristocratic form, the principle of social life is virtue, which James Sellers has recently para-
phrased in more modern language as "willed initiative."

In a democracy there is no prince furnished with an army to
maintain the laws by force. And since the people are established on the basis of parity, there is no pride of rank to
exploit. If there is any will or motivation to see that the laws
are obeyed and that justice is done, it must come out of the

hearts of the citizenry, from the will and ability of the people to act on behalf of the greater community. It is this quality, rather than fear or ambition, that makes things work in a democracy. This quality is *la vertu*. . . . It conveys the idea that the citizen of a republic finds the beginning of his participation in governance in his own inner spirit, but that this spirit takes the form of action, and especially that kind of action that expresses willingness: initiative.[26]

In Montesquieu's analysis, a republic will stand only so long as its citizens love it. If it needs external coercion its principle is lost. And Montesquieu, echoing many a hero of the early Roman republic, tells us that only frugality and the absence of luxury can keep the public interest in the minds of the citizens and make possible that renunciation of self which is so difficult but without which no republic can long survive. The agrarian ideal of Jefferson and others in the early republic—the ideal of a nation of frugal independent husbandmen ready to serve at their community's call—owes much to this notion of republican virtue. Although from a different starting point, the evangelical version of the Protestant Ethic led to an identical conclusion.

In the end the Roman archetypes proved less profound and less lasting than the biblical ones for Latin culture was more confined to the elite than biblical culture. The great image for the founding of the nation was Exodus, not Aeneid. Even the classicist Jefferson proposed a picture of Moses leading Israel across the Red Sea for the Great Seal of the United States. And in his second inaugural address he said, "I need, too, the favor of that Being in whose hands we are, who led our forefathers, as Israel of old, from their native land, and planted them in a country flowing with all the necessaries and comforts of life; who has covered our infancy with his providence, and our riper years with his wisdom and power."[27]

We might wonder at the choice of Israel and Rome as the archetypes of the new nation, in view of the long history of suffering of the former and the decline and fall of the latter. We may wonder that our ancestors over-looked the darker days of those earlier nations. They did not. They hoped to construct a republic on principles so sound that it might avoid their fate. But they were certain that if we should decline in piety and public virtue we would meet the inexorable fate of the nations, which are as but dust in the hands of God.

12

But there was another tradition of political thought also beginning to seep into the American colonies in the early 18th century, one related to Calvinist theology and classical philosophy in curious patterns of attraction and repulsion. This was a relatively new trend of thought originating in the first attempt to apply the attitudes and orientations of natural science to the social and political sphere when, in the 17th century, natural science began to take on the prestige that it has characteristically main-tained ever since. The truly innovative figure here was Thomas Hobbes although it was the more modest and conciliatory thought of Hobbes's follower and critic, John Locke, that had most influence in America. As many scholars have pointed out there is a remarkable resem-blance between Hobbes's state of nature and Augus-tine's *civitas terrena*. Both assume that natural man is fun-damentally selfish and greedy, eager to satisfy his own desires and ready to dominate or destroy any who stand in his way. The *bellum omnium contra omnes* is Hobbes's phrase, but it is an apt description of Augustine's picture of man without God. Just as Augustine's *cupiditas* as the principle of the earthly city is an appropriate term for Hobbes's conception of fundamental human motivation. The critical difference between the two theorists—and it is important because it will distinguish Calvinist from utilitarian in 18th-century America—becomes evident when we consider how each of them explained such order and peace as does prevail in worldly society.

For both Augustine and Hobbes the *bellum omnium* is a marginal case, illustrative of certain truths about human nature but not, except in situations of exceptional breakdown, actually descriptive of normal human existence. For Augustine, of course, God is lord of the earthly city as well as the heavenly one. His providence, even though inscrutable, orders human history. Among other things, he often chooses to send kings and tyrants, including unjust ones, as a scourge to the wicked and a trial to the saints, and such kings maintain a semblance of peace. But essential to Augustine's political thought is the idea that even fallen men retain some "image" or "impression" of divine truth and justice, without which there could be no political order.[28]

What distinguishes Hobbes from the classical and Christian traditions and their modern continuers is the absence of any notion of God or the Good and a corresponding radical theoretical individualism. For Hobbes the marginal case of the war of all against all is not escaped through any semblance or trace of divine justice but through a social compact made by individuals to maximize their self-interest. In order to evade the natural state of anxiety, fear, and suffering, men appoint a monarch over themselves to whom they cede their natural liberty in return for peace and security. But for Hobbes, and here Locke is his true disciple, social concord is still based not on divine justice, not even on a shadow of *caritas*, but on self-interest, on *cupiditas* alone.

The idea that society could be based on a mere coagulation of individual interests, that the pursuit of private vice could result in public virtue, was a radically new idea in the 17th and 18th centuries and one that did not sit well with other still powerful traditions.

13

The remarkable coherence of the American revolutionary movement and its successful conclusion in the constitution of a new civil order are due in considerable part to the convergence of the Puritan covenant pattern and the Montesquieuan republican pattern. The former was represented above all by New England, the latter by Virginia, but both were widely diffused in the consciousness of the colonial population. Both patterns saw society resting on the deep inner commitment of its members, the former through conversion, the latter through republican virtue. Both saw government as resting on law, which, in its positive form, was created by the active participation of those subject to it, yet ultimately derives from some higher source, either God or Nature. When Jefferson evoked at the beginning of the Declaration of Independence the "laws of nature and of nature's God" he was able to fuse the ultimate legitimating principles of both traditions. And when in concluding it he wrote, "And for the support of this declaration, with a firm reliance on the protection of divine providence, we mutually pledge to each other our lives, our fortunes, and our sacred honor," he was not only invoking a republican formula for the establishment of a civil compact but echoing the formula of the Puritan covenant. Only the confluence of these two patterns can help us understand the fusion of passion and reason that, with such consistency, seems to have motivated the major actors in the revolutionary drama.

Liberty was the great theme of American revolutionary emotion. As early as 1770 one observer noted that "the minds of the people are wrought up into as high a degree of Enthusiasm by the word liberty, as could have been expected had Religion been the cause."[29] Liberty meant liberation from British tyranny and from the rule of kings. It is hard for us to realize the psychological exhilaration of the overthrow of monarchy in that day when, except for a few small and declining republics, monarchy was universal. In view of the fact that Parliament more than George III was tyrannizing over the Americans it is remarkable that it was George who became the very symbol and incarnation of the restraint the Americans were overthrowing. In the imagination of some New England preachers George even became the Antichrist, the "horrible wild beast" of the 13th Book of Revelation.[30] The intensity of the rejection of the king, considering the fact that he was a constitutional monarch and, in any dispassionate use of the term, no tyrant, is only to be explained as the rejection of a whole conception of authority, that is of authority as external, arbitrary constraint, for which a king is a much better image than a parliament.

In the first months of the war a spontaneous unity swept through the colonies. David Ramsay in his history of the revolution published in 1791 looked back at the spirit of 1775 as one that "calmer seasons can scarcely credit." He wrote:

The Governor of the Universe, by a sacred influence on their minds, disposed them to union. From whatever cause it proceeded, it is certain, that a disposition to do, to suffer, and to accomodate, spread from breast to breast, and from colony to colony, beyond the reach of human calculation.[31]

The "brotherly affection," the willingness to "abridge ourselves of our superfluities, for the supply of others necessities," that Winthrop spoke of in the early Puritan covenant seemed again to live in the revolutionary ranks. The liberation from external restraint and the emergence of "the blessed unison of the whole American harpsichord, as now set to the tune of liberty," as it was described in 1775, must indeed have inspired the millenial expectations that were never very far below the surface in colonial America.[32]

Yet the difficult years of 1777 and 1778 saw much falling away, doubting, and hardness of heart. One Calvinist minister was led to produce a sermon called "The American States Acting Over the Part of the Children of Israel in the Wilderness and Thereby Impeding Their Entrance into Canaan's Rest."[33]

The spirit of 1775 that Alan Heimert has compared so convincingly to that of the Great Awakening, had not been able to survive genuine adversity or overcome the selfish proclivities or inordinate demands of individuals. Even in 1775, John Adams recounted, ". . . a common horse jockey . . . who was always in the law, and had been sued in many actions at almost every court," came up to him and said, "Oh, Mr. Adams what great things have you and your colleagues done for us! We can never be grateful enough to you. There are no courts of justice now in the province, and I hope there never will another."[34] Adams's distress at this homegrown anarchism that Edwards and Backus had noticed earlier was motivated at least in part by class anxieties and concern for the protection of property, though he was also moved by larger purposes. But the dissenting Protestants of all classes were equally alarmed after 1776 about the absence of governmental regularity. They repeatedly requested the Massachusetts General Court, for example, to establish a constitution so that the people of the commonwealth would not be left "in a state of nature," by which they meant, with Jonathan Edwards, "*Hobb's* state of war," where men "would act as the wild beast of the desert; prey upon and destroy one another,"[35] We are not surprised to learn that Alexander Hamilton said, "We may preach till we are tired of the theme the necessity of disinterestedness in republics, without making a single proselyte." But Jefferson did not much disagree when he wrote at the end of the war, "They will forget themselves, but in the sole faculty of making money, and will never think of uniting to effect a due respect for their rights."[36]

14

To some extent this tension between concern for the common cause and concern for one's selfish interest was reflected at the theoretical level in the tension between utilitarians and those who held the traditional religious and philosophical views. There were some Americans in the 18th century fully aware of the underlying conflict. In his *Two Discourses on Liberty* of 1774, Nathaniel Niles, the Calvinist preacher and follower of Jonathan Edwards, attacked Locke's view of the origin and purpose of government. The notion that government arises out of a contract for the mutual defense of private property "is the maxim on which pirates and gangs of robbers live in a kind of unity," he wrote. He correctly pointed out that the utilitarian conception of society, lacking even the Augustinian trace of divine order, would inevitably collapse into chaos:

God cements mankind into society for their greater good, while each, consenting to submit his exercise of the several powers with which he is vested to the cognizance of the whole body, agrees to deny himself such gratifications as are deemed incompatible with the felicity of the rest. . . . Just so far as his affection is turned on private interest, he will become regardless of the common good, and when he is detached from the community in heart, his services will be very precarious at best, and those will not be expected at all which imply self-denial.[37]

The conscious conflict between the civil (Calvinist, classical) and utilitarian views came to a head, then, over the issue of whether virtue or interest was to be the effective basis of the new American polity. In the 1770s most articulate Americans chose virtue. In arguing against a property qualification for holding office, an anonymous tract of 1776 argued:

So sure as we make interest necessary in this case, as sure we root out virtue; and what will then become of the genuine principle of freedom. This notion of an interest has the direct-est tendency to set up the avaricious over the head of the poor, though the latter are ever so virtuous.[38]

Samuel Adams, who hoped America would be a "Christian Sparta," expressed the general view when he wrote:

We may look up to Armies for our Defence, but Virtue is our best Security. It is not possible that any State shd long remain free, where Virtue is not supremely honord.[39]

But by the 1790s, as Gordon S. Wood has shown, quite other views were beginning to prevail. Instead of lamenting the fact that Americans seemed to be more intent on individual happiness than upon public good, some began to argue that just such a principle was the basis of the new American system. The new Constitution, it was felt, harnessed individual acquisitiveness to public order. As James Wilson wrote, in America there was introduced "into the very form of government, such particular checks and controls, as to make it advantageous even for bad men to act for the public good." Wood sums up these views as follows:

America would remain free not because of any quality in its citizens of spartan self-sacrifice to some nebulous public good, but in the last analysis because of the concern each individual would have in his own self-interest and personal freedom.[40]

Wilson and others entranced with the new system argued that it would be immune to the corruptions of the classical republics and that it would not suffer a collapse into tyranny. John Adams, who believed virtue was essential in a republic but saw awfully little of it in his countrymen, adopted a very somber view of America's future and interpreted the Constitution largely in negative terms as an effort to slow the inevitable descent.[41] Just as Locke did not displace Calvin in the 17th century so the newer view did not eliminate the older one in the late 18th century. Washington's Farewell Address, published in 1796, restated the older moral position when he argued that Providence connects "the permanent felicity of a Nation with its virtue," and the early 19th century would see a revival of those sentiments in both religious and political form. The struggle of the two positions has never ceased and the conflict between them is a central theme of this book.[42]

The founding fathers as they moved from heroic acts of liberation to the constituting of liberty were aware of the difficulty of maintaining revolutionary zeal as the basis for civil responsibility. Revolution and constitution are as necessarily interlinked as are conversion and covenant, their lineal predecessors, but the tension between them seems as inevitable in the one case as in the other. The Constitution could not take for granted that its citizens would all be motivated by civic virtue and so its concern was as much to protect individuals and groups from abuse at the hands of the government and their fellow citizens as it was to involve all its citizens in genuine participation. Indeed many delegates at the Constitutional Convention feared the active participation of the ordinary citizens far more than their lack of zeal. The Constitution, therefore, was a kind of "external covenant" uniting convinced republicans with the lukewarm —as perhaps it had to be.

The men who consciously felt themselves to be "founding fathers" had a profound conviction of the solemnity and significance of their role as lawgivers. John Adams wrote that he was grateful to have "been sent into life at a time when the greatest lawgivers of antiquity would have wished to live."[43] The time, care, and enormous intelligence expended on the process of producing the Constitution expressed not only the traditional culture of a covenant- and compact-making people, perhaps unique in that respect in human history, but also a sense of the meaning of their act on the world stage. John Adams, even ten years before the Revolution, could write: "I always consider the settlement of America as the opening of a grand scheme and design in Providence for the illumination of the ignorant and the emancipation of the slavish part of mankind all over the earth."[44] At the end of the 17th and the beginning of the 18th centuries Americans had wavered about claiming to be a city set on a hill with the eyes of the world upon it. But by the end of the 18th they were certain once more. In Washington's first inaugural address, occurring at the event that completed, as it were, the constituting of the new nation, he said: "The preservation of the sacred fire of liberty and the destiny of the republican model of government are justly considered, perhaps, as *deeply*, as *finally,* staked on the experiment intrusted to the hands of the American people." They created a structure that, within limits we will have to consider, did protect the liberty of the people and did provide a space for popular initiative. In that, the founding fathers were not deluded in their conviction of the importance of their acts.

Perhaps it would be well to make more explicit the analogy between revolution and constitution on the one hand and conversion and covenant on the other that underlies this whole discussion. Revolution, like conversion, is an act of liberation, a leaving of old structures, a movement away from constraint. Both revolution and conversion open up the deepest levels of the psyche, touch the springs of our deepest hopes and fears. If these acts of liberation did not contain elements of antinomianism and anarchism they would not be genuine, for the old authority must be radically broken before the new order can be born. But unless the free act of liberation moves rapidly toward an act of institution or constitution, an act not of throwing off the past but of establishing the future, then even the liberation itself turns into its opposite. Conversion that does not move toward covenant becomes a new hardness of heart. Revolution that does not move toward constitution quickly becomes a new despotism, as we have seen with so many 19th and 20th-century "revolutions." It is in this sense that the American Revolution succeeded, where so many others failed.

And yet the success it had was at best partial. The Constitution was after all an external covenant. To Jefferson and the evangelicals, perhaps those most concerned that the element of liberation not be lost in the act of institution, the establishment of the Constitution was only the beginning instead of the end of the struggle. Jefferson, as is well known, believed that every generation had the right "to begin the world over again," and that: "Nothing is unchangeable but the inherent and unalienable rights of man," and it was he that felt it would be a good thing to have a revolution every 20 years.[45] He was contemptuous of those who "look at constitutions with sanctimonious reverence, and deem them like the ark of the covenant, too sacred to be touched."[46] The evangelicals, in the revival of 1800 that was intimately connected with the electoral victory of Jeffersonian republicanism called for a "SECOND REVOLUTION, which is inward and spiritual."[47] Like Edwards they wanted everyone in a full covenant and would be satisfied with nothing less. For the Jeffersonians and evangelicals a constitution too quickly becomes cold and external, a shell for the pursuit of self-interest rather than a space for the exercise of free initiative in the public interest.

Thus the tensions that had long operated in America's religious life were transferred into American political life. A structure of liberty, necessary as it is to prevent liberation from destroying itself, nevertheless contains within it new forms of external constraint and new bulwarks for private interest. It requires therefore, again and again, just as religious life requires reformation and revival, a new birth of freedom.

II

America as a
Chosen People

AMERICA, like Canaan, was not uninhabited
when God's new Israel arrived on these shores.
Yet in the last chapter we described "America's Myth of
Origin" without ever mentioning the fact that the American Indians were rich in origin myths and that many
Indian peoples had elaborate ritual cycles deriving from
those origin myths, cycles such as are still being per-
formed by the Navaho and Pueblo Indians today. The
great dream in which the early settlers lived had entirely
Middle Eastern and European roots and had nothing
whatever to do with native American culture except inso-
far as man's mythic life everywhere shares certain general themes.

For a long time, indeed for centuries, the new settlers
failed to appreciate the fact that the people they found
here lived in a different dream. Whether the Indian was
seen as noble or as horrid savage, he was treated as if he
were a character in the European's dream, as if he had
no dream of his own. Only recently has the vast archaic
symbolism of Indian mythology begun to be ap-
preciated, and lately even perceived as a source of
spiritual life for all Americans. This failure to see the

Indians in their own terms was only the cultural side of a denial of humanity that was also expressed in economic and even biological terms. The Indians were deprived by the new settlers, not only of the inherent human right to have one's culture understood and respected, but they were ruthlessly deprived of land and livelihood and all too often of life itself. This was the primal crime on which American society is based.

In the first decades of settlement the primal crime was compounded with another enormity. Still other peoples living outside the European dream—Africans, with their own immense cosmological symbolism—were forced to become actors in the European dream under the most tragic circumstances possible. To the expropriation and extermination of the Indian was added the forcible transportation of the African Negro out of his own land and his enslavement in America. Thus at the very beginning of American society there was a double crime, the incalculable consequences of which still stalk the land. We must ask what in the dream of white America kept so many for so long, so many even at this day, from seeing any crime at all. For that we need to consider the ambiguities of chosenness.

2

An extreme example will put the issue sharply. Senator Albert J. Beveridge delivered a speech on the floor of the United States Senate shortly after his return from a tour of the Philippines in January 1900. He referred to the wealth of the islands and their importance to the United States, to the indolence of the natives and their incapacity for self-government, and to the war of subjugation which the United States Army was then waging against the Filipino independence movement. The American opposition to that war, he said, in terms we have become familiar with in late years, was "the chief factor in prolonging it." Warming to his subject he laid down the justification for annexation in the following words:

God has not been preparing the English-speaking and Teutonic peoples for a thousand years for nothing but vain and idle self-contemplation and self-admiration. No. He made us master organizers of the world to establish system where chaos reigned. He has given us the spirit of progress to overwhelm the forces of reaction throughout the earth. He has made us adept in government that we may administer government among savage and senile peoples. Were it not for such a force as this the world would relapse into barbarism and night. And of all our race He has marked the American people as His chosen nation to finally lead in the redemption of the world.[1]

Even though the biblical imagery has been muddied over with 19th-century racism, a subject to which we will return, we can see in grotesquely heightened form precisely the arguments used to justify American treatment of Indians and blacks from the very beginning.

Senator Beveridge was no ignorant "red neck." As United States Senators go he was rather better educated and more intellectual than most. But similar sentiments are to be found in Americans of far greater capacity than he. Fifty years earlier Herman Melville, one of the handful of writers of the first magnitude that America has produced, could write as follows:

Escaped from the house of bondage, Israel of old did not follow after the ways of the Egyptians. To her was given an express dispensation; to her were given new things under the sun. And we Americans are the peculiar, chosen people—the Israel of our time; we bear the ark of the liberties of the world. Seventy years ago we escaped from thrall; and, besides our first birthright—embracing one continent of earth—God has given to us, for a future inheritance, the broad domains of the political pagans, that shall yet come and lie down under the shade of our ark, without bloody hands being lifted. God has predestined, mankind expects, great things from our race; and great things we feel in our souls. The rest of the nations must soon be in our rear. We are the pioneers of the world; the advance-guard, sent on through the wilderness of untried things, to break a new path in the New World that is ours. In our youth is our strength; in our inexperience, our wisdom. At a period when other nations have but lisped, our deep voice is heard afar. Long enough have we been sceptics with regard to ourselves, and doubted whether, indeed, the political Messiah had come. But he has come in *us*, if we would but give utterance to his promptings. And let us always remember that with ourselves, almost for the first time in the history of earth, national selfishness is unbounded philanthropy; for we cannot do a good to America, but we give alms to the world.[2]

Not many years ago we had a Secretary of Defense who believed that what is good for General Motors is good for America. Melville seemed to believe that what is good for America is good for the world. In such a passage we can see the link between the notion of the American Israel, which was already in the mind of John Winthrop in the early 17th century, and Henry Luce's recent idea of "the American Century," or John Foster Dulles's easy identification of the "free world" with those nations willing to do the bidding of the American government.

3

To speak of the ambiguities of chosenness is to indicate that the image is complex, that it accounts for much of the best in America as well as the worst. To begin to see some of the positive implications of chosenness we may consider an address entitled "Our Country's Place

in History" given by Rabbi Isaac M. Wise in Cincinnati
in 1869 some 20 years after the passage from Melville
was written and 30 years before the speech of Senator
Beveridge. While it has echoes of both it also sounds
other notes, some of which we discerned in the last chapter. After briefly describing the history of liberty in
Europe and its practice by the Puritans he came to the
American Revolution:

Glory to the memory of the heroes of the revolution, to the
generous godfathers of liberty. Glory to the memory of
George Washington and his heroic compatriots. They were
the chosen instruments in the hands of Providence, to turn the
wheel of events in favor of liberty forever; and they proved
worthy of their great mission, of their immortal work. . . . The
millions of oppressed men and women in all countries, whose
chains have been broken and whose prisons have been razed,
are the grand chorus, who sing the praise of the American
revolution. . . . The framers of the Constitution were wise
enough to confront the destiny of the nation, and honest
enough to express their full conviction in the paragraphs of
the Constitution and its immortal preamble. The people of the
United States, on accepting this Constitution, had formally
and solemnly chosen its destiny, to be now and forever the
palladium of liberty and its divinely appointed banner-bearer,
for the progress and redemption of mankind.[3]

While in these lines Rabbi Wise accepts the redemp-
tive role of America that both Melville and Beveridge
asserted, he does not see it as taking effect through political sway over pagans or over savage and senile races, but
through an example set for "the millions of oppressed
men and women in all countries."

Again, like Melville and Beveridge, Rabbi Wise sees
Americans as a "peculiar people," but their peculiarity
does not rest in their being of Anglo-Saxon race but

rather, in his words, because they are a "conflux of the various families of man." "We are," he said, "originally English, Irish, French, Dutch, German, Polish, Spanish, or Scandinavian; but we are neither. We are Americans. Every child born on this soil is Americanized. Our country has a peculiar people to work out a new and peculiar destiny."[4] The notion of Americanization, that Rabbi Wise is already using in 1869, will require further examination, but it is not obvious that he means by it the domination of one American group over all the others.

Finally, near the end of his talk, Rabbi Wise sounds another note that was not evident in the passages from Melville and Beveridge, though we will see that Melville in this respect later changed his mind. Rabbi Wise said:

Nothing can arrest our progress, nothing drag our country down from her high place in history, except our own wickedness working a wilful desertion of our destiny, the desertion from the ideal of liberty. As long as we cling to this ideal, we will be in honor, glory, wealth and prosperity.[5]

In Rabbi Wise's version of the old idea of covenant there is the notion that our chosenness is not absolute but conditional, that it involves a choice on our part. Remaining faithful to the ideal of liberty is his version of John Winthrop's Deuteronomic injunction, "Let us choose life."

4

The notion that the Americans are an especially choice and chosen people can be found from the earliest times. In early 17th-century Virginia John Rolfe could refer to the colonists as "a peculiar people, marked and chosen by the hand of God,"[6] and in late 17th century William Stoughton of Massachusetts could say, "God sifted a whole nation that he might send choice grain over into the wilderness."[7] This way of thinking reached a perfect crescendo at the time of the Revolution when America was referred to as God's "first-born nation," and speculation on the special world-historical meaning of American independence became almost a national obsession. But although elements of self-congratulation and self-righteousness were never missing they were usually muted by the conditional covenant context of the assertions. The "choice seed" in the Wilderness was from the beginning felt to be subject to "wilderness temptations."[8] The jeremiad or denunciation of the sins of the people was an integral part of early New England culture, as Perry Miller has pointed out.[9] The sins denounced were, for the most part, the conventional sins of Protestantism; sabbath-breaking and profanity were more apt to be mentioned than anything to do with the treatment of Indians and blacks. Denunciations of acquisitiveness, sharply observant of current practices, were not lacking. Increase Mather, for example, could write in 1676:

Land! Land! hath been the Idol of many in *New-England:* whereas the first Planters here that they might keep themselves together were satisfied with one Acre for each person, as his propriety, and after that with twenty Acres for a Family, how have Men since coveted after the earth, that many hundreds, nay thousands of Acres, have been engrossed by one man, and they that profess themselves Christians, have forsaken Churches, and Ordinances, and all for land and elbow-room enough in the world. *Lot* would forsake the Land of *Canaan*, and the Church, . . . that he might have better worldly accomodations in Sodome.[10]

But Increase was equally scandalized by vanity of hair style or dress, loitering in taverns, and early departure from public worship. Whether the sins denounced seem trivial to us or not the continuous denunciation of them by the Puritan ministers and their insistence that God's blessing could become a curse unless the people reformed kept alive the idea that divine judgment hangs over even an elect people and helped to prevent national self-worship. It will become apparent in the next chapter that such Puritan moralism, even at its best, exacted a heavy price.

It was inevitable that the religious fervor about liberty, which reached a climax at the time of the Revolution, would raise doubts about slavery. Well before the Revolution, Quakers had begun the first systematic opposition to slavery with an effort to abolish it within their own ranks. By the time of the Revolution, evangelicals and Calvinists generally shared these views. A feeling began to develop that slavery was so serious a sin that divine retribution of a peculiarly appropriate kind might ensue. Already in 1768 the Reverend Francis Alison in Philadelphia wrote to Ezra Stiles, "I am assured the Common father of all men will severely plead a Controversy against these Colonies for Enslaving Negros, and keeping their children, born British subjects, in perpetual slavery—and possibly for this wickedness God threatens us with slavery." In 1774, with war already at hand, the Danbury town meeting in Connecticut declared that ". . . we have great reason to apprehend the enslaving the *Africans* is one of the crying sins of our land, for which Heaven is now chastising us."[11] The whole issue is beautifully summed up by Dr. Benjamin Rush who, in his *Address upon Slave-keeping* advised the clergy to "Remember that national crimes require national punishments, and without declaring what punishment awaits this evil, you may venture to assure them, that it cannot pass with impunity, unless God shall cease to be just or merciful."[12]

In spite of these sentiments, the will to liberate the slaves, part of the general revolutionary impulse toward liberation, faltered during the Constitutional Convention. Outside the South abolition was rather quickly enacted at the state level, but in the federal Constitution all that could be gained in the compromises leading to the final draft was the prohibition of the importation of slaves after 1808. Even though to many the toleration of slavery in the Constitution was sure evidence that it was but an external covenant, the creation of a viable national structure and its defense against foreign incursion so preoccupied the new nation that it was not until nearly forty years after the Constitution was adopted that the issue of slavery would once again come to the fore.

5

The Roman facade of the new republic was singularly cold and unhomelike to the great majority of the American population. There was a brief flurry of republican religion, a stoic, rational deism conforming to the limits of pure reason and advocating civic virtue. But outside an assortment of upper-class Virginia and New England aristocrats, and avant-garde radicals like Tom Paine, it had no appeal. Jefferson's prediction that Unitarianism would soon become the American religion could not have been more wrong. Even he turned to biblical imagery when he wished to invoke powerful symbols to express the national experience, and he was himself embraced as a symbol by those whose religious fervor he could never understand. When that second American revolution, inward and spiritual, broke in 1800 it was evangelical and revivalist. It was the beginning of the Second Great Awakening and it carried all before it, determining the direction of the popular consciousness for the rest of the century. It is essential that we understand the relation between a renewed Protestant piety and a gradually clarifying American national consciousness if we are to grasp the meaning of American myth and symbol in the 19th century and our inheritance from it.

In a sense the deistic symbolism remained embalmed at the level of the civil religion, since it was above all Washington, Adams, Jefferson, and Madison who set the tone of the national cult. Public proclamation tended even to avoid the word God, referring instead to "Providence," "that Infinite Power which rules the destinies of the universe," "that Being in whose hands we are," and so forth. Above all every hint of sectarian specificity was avoided in the religious symbolism that was so evident in American political life from the earliest days of the republic. That this symbolism could survive the passing of those whose private religious and philosophical mood it expressed can be explained only by the deeply held doctrine of religious liberty, enshrined in the First Amendment prohibition of the establishment of religion. Americans were a religious people and their public life ever gave expression to that fact, but they avoided any hint of establishment by opting for a neutral religious language that could give offense to none.

By the same token that neutral deistic language warmed the hearts of none and by itself and unaided, it could hardly have provided the imaginative basis of a national consciousness without which the new nation could easily have shattered into the divisions and fragments that continually threatened it. What civil religion unaided could not accomplish became possible with the help of a burgeoning revivalism. Cold external forms could be filled with a warm inner life, appropriated and impressed into the imaginative life of the people. It is precisely this dynamic combination of public form and private meaning that makes the American civil religion so difficult to understand and analyze. Its severe formal limits have made it difficult to manipulate by public officials. Only the greatest presidents have given it a personal impress: Washington by his role as liberator and his great refusal to exercise the role of Caesar; Lincoln by his martyrdom; Jefferson through language, more in the Declaration of Independence than in any of his state papers; and Lincoln again, especially in the Second Inaugural and the Gettysburg Address. But behind those great gestures and proclamations there is no orthodox interpreter, no government-supported school of civil theology, no censor with power to forbid what does not conform. The meaning, the inner meaning, is left to private interpretation, to the speech of any man— preacher, politician, or poet—who has the power to persuade.[13] The result was not consensus—there have always been sharp cleavages as to the deepest meaning of America—but not anarchy either.

On the great issues of the 19th century—slavery or freedom, public good or private gain—it was the churches that spoke with the combined voice of believers and citizens, even when deeply divided among themselves. Perry Miller begins his history of *The Life of the Mind in America* with a 90-page section entitled "The Evangelical Basis," and William McLoughlin has written: "The history of American Evangelicalism is then more than a history of a religious movement. To understand it is to understand the whole temper of American life in the nineteenth century."[14] There is no other way to understand the American sense of chosenness and the American sense of judgment, even though long before 1900 other voices were beginning to make themselves heard.

6

There are linear continuities between the churches of the colonial period and those of the early 19th century but the mood is undeniably different. In the colonial period whole communities and churches often came over from Europe together. Religious community, whatever it might be lacking in actuality, was at least potentially present. The First Great Awakening took the parish as its basic unit. The preaching of Edwards was addressed to individuals within an established communal framework; it was his job to help in the conversion and transformation of men, not in the establishment of institutions. In the period of enormous expansion to the West after independence the situation was quite different. It was the role of evangelists in the Second Great Awakening after 1800 not only to convert individuals but to inspire communities so that they might establish and transform institutions.

Out of the flotsam and jetsam of the pious and the reprobate who filled the cities and towns of the West there had to be woven an entire associational life capable of carrying on the daily social functions, and social institutions had not merely to be established but uplifted and improved. Ultimately the aim of the revival was not local at all. A writer in the *Christian Spectator* in 1829 said that the Gospel not only can rescue individuals, "it can renew the face of communities and nations. The same heavenly influence which, in revivals of religion, descends on families and villages . . . may in like manner, when it shall please him who hath the residue of the Spirit, descend to refresh and beautify a whole land."[15] The increasingly elaborated techniques of the revivalists for reaching into the deepest level of unconscious motivation in the common man were to be used not only as an aid to open him to the infusion of divine grace, but to make him a citizen. To quote the *Christian Spectator* again: " 'What has religion to do with the State?' you ask. In the form of ecclesiastical alliances, nothing; but in its operation as a controlling, purifying power in the consciences of the people, we answer, it has everything to do, it is the last hope of republics."[16]

Tocqueville and other Europeans were quick to notice how difficult it was to discern the machinery of government in much of America. Even bureaucrats, not to mention army and police, were seldom visible. As a student of Montesquieu, Tocqueville was aware that where the inner control of religious discipline operates the external compulsion of the state is not necessary. But Tocqueville was also aware that the political operation of religion in America was different from that conceived by many 18th-century philosophers, for here religion was not controlled by a hierarchy of priests monopolizing the dispensing of sacraments and the interpretation of dogma. Rather religion itself was "democratic and republican," submitting "the truths of the other world to private judgement."[17] What he did not see so well is that the great engine for maintaining the effectiveness of religion in national life was not dogma at all but revivalism, intense, immediate, and personal.

It is easy for those educated in the 20th century to believe that religion is a form of ideology in Mannheim's classic sense of the term, that it operates as a support for an existing order rather than as a utopia to undercut it. But the total applicability of that analysis is doubtful at any period of American history and never more doubtful than in the first half of the 19th century. The millennialism of the American Protestant tradition again and again spawned movements for social change and social reform, held forth a utopia of the Kingdom of God on earth that undercut any simple commitment to the status quo. Evangelical religion contributed to the growth of a national consciousness that cannot be understood wholly in terms of classic liberal theory. America was not simply a neutral legal state within which the individual could rationally pursue his self-interest. Nor was the questioning of existing institutional arrangements only the protest of those whose interests were violated. The motivation of those who initiated the great antislavery crusade that we are about to consider, was far less any direct or indirect economic self-interest than it was millennial republican idealism. I do not wish to imply that self-interest, any more than naked political force, was ever absent in American society. Where voluntary participation in the social process was barred—as among the slaves in the South, among the Indians along the frontiers, and later in the 19th century among the urban poor —the application of police, quasi-police, and military force was often violent and brutal. And among the majority population self-interest was intertwined with idealism in deep and complex ways as we shall see further in the next chapter. But the meaning of the American experience will remain forever opaque to those who, once they see through the most simple-minded version of American idealism, can find only violence and self-interest in its stead.

7

However intertwined with other issues it gradually became, the antislavery movement in the 19th century came primarily out of the religious and national energies that we have been discussing. Carried on even in the relatively quiet early years of the republic by Quakers, antislavery agitation became intense after 1830 among such groups as the Baptists in New England and a wide

assortment of evangelical Churches west of the Alleghe-
nies. The two great spokesmen of the movement, William Lloyd Garrison in New England and Theodore
Dwight Weld in Ohio, were almost archetypal combina-
tions of revivalist preacher and Old Testament prophet.
The tensions between the two men reveal much about
the cultural life of the day.

William Lloyd Garrison was the most stalwart and uncompromising, if sometimes sectarian and isolated, of
the abolitionists. He is important for his unrelenting
propaganda and for his remorseless unmasking of
American pretentions. Unwilling to accept the arguments of the more moderate—that slavery was a mere
blot on an otherwise noble American countenance, a
blemish that was not indicative of its essential quality—
Garrison found slavery an evil so profound that it called
all American self-conceptions in question. Ridiculing
Washington's notion that the establishment of America
was an "experiment" on which the fate of the world
depends, in 1837 Garrison wrote,

As if God had suspended the fate of all nations, and hazarded
the fulfilment of his glorious promises, upon the result of a
wild and cruel "experiment" by a land-stealing, blood-thirsty,
man-slaying and slave-trading people in one corner of the
globe! As if God could not easily dash this nation in pieces, as
a potter's vessel is broken, and thereby vindicate his eternal
justice. . . .[18]

Working entirely within the symbolism and rhetoric of
the civil religion, he yet turned it into an instrument of
searing denunciation of national pride when finally he
was driven to denounce the Constitution itself, because
it allowed slavery to continue, as "a covenant with death
and an agreement with hell,"[19] In 1854, in a gesture with

which we have latterly become familiar, he publicly burned a copy of it, and later withdrew into bitter aloofness. In the last years before the Civil War, Garrison's splinter of the antislavery movement was almost without direct political effect, but the witness of radical intransigence made its own contribution.

Theodore Weld, coming out of the turbulent West, was a convert of Charles Grandison Finney, the greatest of all American evangelists. Keeping considerably closer to the main stream than Garrison, Weld's great contribution to the antislavery movement was his transformation of revivalist techniques into instruments of the abolitionist cause. His appeal was neither to interest nor even to duty but to warm emotional conversion. Speaking in 1834 to those he hoped would join his band of young men battling for the abolitionist cause, he asked for "hearts and heads and tongues—for faith and works." The tone of his appeal can be glimpsed in the following words:

If your hearts ache and bleed, we want you, you will help us; but if you merely adopt our principles as dry theories, do let us alone: we have millstones enough swinging at our necks already. Further, if you join us merely out of a sense of *duty*, we pray you keep aloof and give place to those who leap into our ranks because they can not keep themselves out; who instead of whining about duty, shout 'privilege,' 'delight'![20]

Time and again in the years 1835 and 1836 Weld went into towns seething with antiabolitionist mobs. Often bruised and injured, often having to stand before a howling mass night after night until, out of exhaustion, he was allowed to speak. One of the great public speakers of his day, Weld many times won over a doubtful or hostile audience. At the end of a passionate exposition of the

necessity of immediate abolition he said, in good revivalist fashion: "Friends, will all of you who believe . . .
please rise to your feet?" The entire audience rose.[21]
While Weld himself moved on, patient coworkers stayed
to organize local societies that would continue the work.
Even more important, Weld and his associates developed a constitutional argument that even as early as
1835 described the treatment in the North of free
Negroes and abolitionists as "denials of rights to the
equal protection of the laws, the safeguards of due process, and the privileges and immunities of citizens," the
very language that would eventually be enshrined in the
Fourteenth Amendment to the Constitution. Unlike Garrison the group around Weld believed that emancipation
was implicit in the Constitution and that what that document needed was not burning but clarification and en-
forcement. Their efforts contributed much to that even-
tual outcome.

I do not deny that there were economic and political
causes of the Civil War and of emancipation or insist
that cultural and religious motives were alone important. I do claim that without those cultural and religious
motives it is not possible to understand what has been
called the Second American Revolution and its outcome
in a new birth of freedom, partial and incomplete though
that outcome, like the first one, was. Sidney Mead has
argued that Abraham Lincoln is "the spiritual center of
American history."[22] Certainly in terms of the dialectic
of covenant and chosenness that we have been discussing in these first two chapters, the Civil War, the event
with which Lincoln is most closely identified, was a kind
of culmination.

8

During the American Revolution, as we have seen, the
traditions of Protestant covenant theology and republi-

can liberty were joined together, but the seam was still highly visible. By the time of the Civil War the fusion was complete, the garment seamless. There were few forms of public expression in early America that could communicate a deeply imaginative symbolism. We never had a tradition of a national theater; and poetry, fiction, and the fine arts were but uncertainly institutionalized by the mid-19th century.[23] Almost the only popular forms with a deep American tradition behind them were the sermon (along with the related form of the political oration) and the hymn. In Lincoln's greatest public statements the tradition of American public oratory, infused with biblical imagery and expressed in an almost Puritan "plain style," attained a classic form. In Julia Ward Howe's "The Battle Hymn of the Republic" the hymn tradition culminated in an almost perfect expression of the national spirit.

The "Battle Hymn" imagery, drawn largely from the Book of Revelation, brings home the apocalyptic character of that moment in the nation's history. It is a time of testing: "He is trampling out the vintage where the grapes of wrath are stored"; and a time of judgment: "He is sifting out the hearts of men before His judgment seat." Christian holiness and republican liberty are finally conjoined: "As he died to make men holy, let us die to make men free." It is not an accident that one of the 20th century's greatest American novels of social protest, *The Grapes of Wrath*, took its title from the second line of the "Battle Hymn" or that the old words took on apocalyptic meaning once again as a rallying cry in the great civil rights demonstrations of the late 1950s and early 1960s. A powerful fusion of imagery and feeling like that in the "Battle Hymn" goes on working down through history.

It is in Lincoln's Second Inaugural Address that we find perhaps the greatest expression of the theme of covenant and judgment in the entire course of American history. It is the final statement on slavery as sin:

> If we shall suppose that American slavery is one of those offenses which, in the providence of God, must needs come, but which, having continued through His appointed time, He now wills to remove, and that He gives to both North and South this terrible war as the woe due to those by whom the offense came, shall we discern therein any departure from those divine attributes which the believers in a living God always ascribe to Him? Fondly do we hope, fervently do we pray, that this mighty scourge of war may speedily pass away. Yet, if God wills that it continue until all the wealth piled up by the bondsman's two hundred and fifty years of unrequited toil shall be sunk, and until every drop of blood drawn with the lash shall be paid by another drawn with the sword, as was said three thousand years ago, so still it must be said "the judgments of the Lord are true and righteous altogether."

And even more significant is Lincoln's insistence in the Gettysburg Address that out of all the blood and the suffering there must come "a new birth of freedom."

The Civil War, like the Revolution, moved from liberation, in this case emancipation of the slaves, to the institution of liberty in the 13th, 14th and 15th Amendments. The most important provisions are contained in the 14th Amendment where Section 1 guaranteed the natural rights of man and equal protection of the laws and Section 5 authorized Congress to enforce these rights. Even though the radical meaning of these clauses was undermined for many decades by narrow court interpretations and a regressive political situation, their meaning can hardly be exaggerated. They are the charter under which many of the advances of the last 20 years have been made. They are the mandate for many more. They altered the role of the national government from one of

largely passive observation in the field of individual
rights to one of active intervention and responsibility.
They give the constitutional legitimation for much that
is still to be realized politically.

9

For all the vitality of the antislavery movement and the
living heritage that it bequeathed us, its success was only
partial and much of what was gained legally was quickly
lost socially and politically. The antislavery movement
was a drama in the white soul. The black American
scarcely emerged on the public stage. With a few exceptions like Frederick Douglass, most of the leaders, even
the most radical—Weld, Garrison, John Brown—were
white. Ex-slaves wrote of their own experiences but the
account of slave life that electrified the country was Har-
riet Beecher Stowe's *Uncle Tom's Cabin.* The whole epic
struggle, as far as most white Americans were concerned,
was one of sin, judgment, and redemption in the white
soul. There was indeed a black epic, and it is now being
recovered. But the black man does not really emerge as
part of the imaginative understanding of white Americans until at least the time of W. E. B. Du Bois, if not
Richard Wright or Malcolm X. Thus fundamental aspects of the American self-picture went unchallenged.
For 50 years after the Civil War that picture was more
self-congratulatory than it had ever been before, its self-
satisfaction reinforced by the image of Lincoln freeing
the slaves, a gesture most magnanimously shared with
black Americans by the practice of naming public schools
in black ghettos after the Great Emancipator.

Far from shaking white Anglo-Saxon self-confidence
the Civil War merely confirmed it and rhetoric of the
kind I quoted from Senator Beveridge at the beginning
of this chapter was all too common in the late years of

the 19th century. In 1885 a Protestant minister, Josiah Strong, later to become one of the founders of the social gospel movement, published a book that became a best seller. Even within this book there is ample evidence of social conscience and yet Strong wrote:

The unoccupied arable lands of the earth are limited and will soon be taken. . . . Then will the world enter upon a new stage of its history—*the final competition of races, for which the Anglo-Saxon is being schooled.* . . . Then this race of unequaled energy, with all the majesty of numbers and the might of wealth behind it—the representative, let us hope, of the largest liberty, the purest Christianity, the highest civilization—having developed peculiarly aggressive traits calculated to impress its institutions upon mankind will spread itself over the earth. . . . Can anyone doubt that the result of this competition of races will be "the survival of the fittest"? . . . Nothing can save the inferior race but a ready and pliant assimilation. . . . The contest is not one of arms, but of vitality and civilization. . . . Is there reasonable room for doubt that this race . . . is destined to dispossess many weaker races, assimilate others, and mold the remainder, until in a very true and important sense it has Anglo-Saxonized mankind.[24]

It is interesting to note how long the Protestant clergyman remains a central spokesman for American culture. Long after Josiah Strong, he would continue to be heard and, in the accents of Bryan and Wilson, the American politician would continue to echo him. Even up to the present day, through men such as Reinhold Niebuhr and Martin Luther King, the tradition continues, although in recent time voices from other quarters are to be heard as well and the Protestant clergyman is less representative. Even before the Civil War, tentatively and often with small audiences, American culture was finding a voice independent of the clergy, beginning to articulate the national consciousness. If we take what D. H. Lawrence referred to as classic American literature or F. O. Matthiessen as the American Renaissance, the first impression may be of how close rather than how far the secular culture was from the Protestant cultural form. Emerson, the fountainhead of the movement, began as a minister and continued to use as his main form the lecture, a transparently secularized version of the sermon. Even in writers such as Thoreau, Melville, and Whitman the influence of the spoken word, the chief idiom of cultivated American literature, is still very strong, but what was being said in that spoken word increasingly contained things that could not be delivered from the Protestant pulpit. After delivering his address to the Harvard Divinity School in 1838 Emerson was not asked to speak again at Harvard for thirty years because his free religious views were so offensive. Thoreau in his essay "Civil Disobedience" could say what all but the most intrepid ministers would hesitate to say: "This people must cease to hold slaves and to make war on Mexico, though it cost them their existence as a people."[25]

Many of the spokesmen of secular culture uttered versions of the doctrine of America as a chosen people that would make a theologian blush, as in the passage from Melville quoted above. But Melville changed his mind and, in a period when he was all but ignored in America, offered one of the most trenchant analyses of the kind of thing Josiah Strong was preaching that has ever been delivered. In his long poem *Clarel*, published in 1876, Melville wrote:

> *As cruel as a Turk:* Whence came
> That proverb old as the crusades?
> From Anglo-Saxons. What are they?
> The Anglo-Saxons—lacking grace

> To win the love of any race;
> Hated by myriads dispossessed
> Of rights—the Indians East and West,
> These pirates of the sphere! grave looters—
> Grave, canting Mammonite freebooters,
> Who in the name of Christ and Trade
> (Oh, bucklered forehead of the brass!)
> Deflower the world's last sylvan glade!

Melville is still enough within the main religious tradition to meditate on the consequences of what seemed to be the new American version of the covenant, without condition or judgment. He says:

> Hypothesise:
> If be a people which began
> Without impediment, or let
> From any ruling where foreran;
> Even striving all things to forget
> But this—the excellence of man
> Left to himself, his natural bent,
> His own devices and intent;
> And if, in satire of the heaven,
> A world, a new world have been given
> For stage whereon to deploy the event;
> If such a people be—well, well,
> One hears the kettledrums of hell!

Finally such a people will foreswear all covenants and speak to God as follows:

> How profits it? And who are Thou
> That we should serve Thee? Of Thy ways
> No knowledge we desire; *new* ways
> We have found out, and better. Go—
> Depart from us . . .

And as a result there would follow what Melville calls the hideous "Dark Ages of Democracy."[26]

The issue of Anglo-Saxon superiority and American imperial destiny came to full public consciousness at the time of the Spanish-American War, especially in the great debate over the annexation of the Philippines. Many, like Senator Beveridge, argued that it was our obligation as a chosen people to bring our blessings to the Filipinos by annexing them. But as the New York Presbyterian minister Henry Van Dyke replied, "If that were true, our whole duty would not be done . . . until we had annexed the misgoverned Spaniards of Spain also. . . . Does the . . . treatment of the Indians in . . . the United States give us a comfortable sense of pride? . . . Is our success in treating the Chinese problem and the Negro problem so notorious that we must attempt to repeat it on a magnified scale eight thousand miles away?" Rather he said we should return to "our unsolved problems staring us in the face, our cities misgoverned and our territories neglected. . . ."[27]

William Vaughn Moody recognized the curse consequent to the broken covenant when he wrote of the same event:

> For save we let the island men go free,
> Those baffled and dislaureled ghosts
> Will curse us from the lamentable coasts
> Where walk the frustrate dead.
> The cup of trembling shall be drainèd quite,
> Even the sour bread of astonishment,
> With ashes of the hearth shall be made white
> Our hair, and wailing shall be in the tent. . . .[28]

And perhaps most succinctly of all, David Starr Jordan, President of Stanford, scoffed at the slogan "The free can conquer but to save" by saying in 1899 that if the Anglo-Saxon "has a destiny incompatible with morality and which cannot be carried out in peace, if he is bound by no pledges and must ride rough shod over the rights and wills of weaker peoples, the sooner he is exterminated the better for the world."[29]

For Garrison, Thoreau, Melville, Moody, and Jordan, and for those Americans for whom they spoke, a conception of chosenness that slips away from the controlling obligations of the covenant is a signpost to hell.

III

Salvation and Success
in America

UP TO this point we have considered a number of
the organizing symbols and mythic elements of
American national consciousness as it developed in the
17th, 18th and 19th centuries. We saw how deeply
rooted the European colonists were in biblical symbolism and how time and again they interpreted their experiences on this continent in terms of biblical archetypes. The pristine newness of the "new world"
seemed to be heavy with an even more radical newness:
the coming of the millennium, the fullness of times,
when God would create a new heaven and a new earth
beginning right here in North America.

A foretaste of that radical consummation was already
attained by those who underwent the experience of conversion that has been so central to every generation of
Protestant Christians in America from the early 17th
century to the present. But conversion was not only a
reward—rebirth into eternal life. It also entailed an obligation—to walk in the ways of the Lord. Those ways were
summed up in the notion of the covenant which linked
the converted men and women, which is to say "new"
men and women, to God. The experience of conversion

and covenant was one of great joy and confirmed a sense of the early Americans that they were an especially choice and chosen people. The boundless energy that has always characterized this people undoubtedly stems in part from this feeling which is similar to that of a child who has been especially favored by its parents. But already in the 17th century the precariousness of the covenant and the blessings flowing from it was sharply experienced. The tendency of the people to walk not in the ways of the Lord but in their own ways, to think not of the general good but of their own private interests, was discerned and condemned by the Puritan ministers. But, even more than they were aware, the colonists had failed the covenant almost before it had been made, for they had founded their new commonwealth on a great crime —the bondage and genocide of other races. The very exclusiveness of their understanding of the covenant had perverted it. Of this we shall have more to say in the next chapter.

The Revolution of the 1770s was preceded by the first great wave of revivals that swept across the colonies in the 1740s. Once again an experience of conversion led into the formation of a covenant, this time the covenant of the new republic. A second great wave of revivals in the early 19th century preceded the Civil War. A renewed experience of divine salvation led to a heightened sense of the imperfections of the national covenant and demanded a nation purged and renewed after the long travail of slavery. Both the Constitution and the Civil War amendments are thoroughly secular documents, but they embody the moral commitment of a covenant people to order its life by the highest standards of which it is capable. As usual their application always fell far short of the aspirations of their drafters. If we are to understand either those aspirations or the failure to attain them, we must continue our effort to understand the nature of this covenant-making people with its deep need for newness and for liberation from oldness in religion, in politics, and in personal life, as well as the moral predicaments the search for newness and liberation so often generated. In the first two chapters we have had much to say of the religious and political nature of our central themes. In this chapter we must look at their personal implications.

We have seen how easily national aggrandizement could slip out of the control of the covenant and become imperialism. We will have to consider how personal aggrandizement could take an analogous route and become aggressive dominance over others in society. In dealing with the perversions of moralism it is easy to become moralistic ourselves. We must remember that the best and the worst in a society or an individual are often closely related. The energy of creation and the energy of aggression are often only a hair's breadth apart. Energy and vitality, which Americans have always had in abundance, are essential in a healthy personality. But that energy, what psychoanalysts sometimes call impulse, must have form, must attain some balance with control, if there is to be maturity of character. It is the role of symbols and myths at the level of personal life both to stimulate and mobilize psychic energy and to provide form and control for it. We will still be talking in this chapter about conversion and covenant, liberation and constitution, but now at the level of personal lives and life histories.

2

Every national character, as Erik Erikson has pointed out, is constructed out of polarities.[1] In America the polarities have been so extreme that they have often seemed impossible to reconcile in a single picture. Americans have been extravagantly praised and blamed as idealists or materialists, anarchists or conformists, the world's most openhanded philanthropists or the world's most efficient killers. These apparent contradictions may be rooted in the basically different motives that brought individuals to America in the first place. They came to find salvation or they came to get rich, or, often enough, for both reasons in some combination not even clear to the individuals themselves. However sharply contradictory these motives might appear, and they have often seemed utterly contradictory, a choice between God and Mammon, or God and the devil, they are at some deep level not unrelated. They can both be considered versions of the same mythic archetype: the quest for paradise; one for an earthly paradise in which impulses are gratified here and now, one for a heavenly paradise at some future time. This dichotomy may be too simple, since in some versions salvation can occur with ecstatic immediacy and the paradise of riches often recedes into a never-never land. But there is little doubt that in the religious culture which is the chrysalis of American myth, the tension between the two motives was conceived as one between worldly pleasures and the hereafter. Perhaps we should begin then with the Puritan version of the problem, since American culture and even American counterculture remain Puritan and moralistic to this day in curious and often disavowed continuity with the 17th century.

We have already seen that John Winthrop in his shipboard sermon of 1630 posed the issue to his congregation as the choice between adhering to God's covenant or pursuing "our carnal intentions seeking great things for ourselves and our posterity," seeking "our pleasures and profits." Clearly stated and often repeated though these alternatives were, there were aspects of Puritanism that made the contrast between them hard to maintain. As everybody knows, the Puritans placed a high value on work in a calling. Building up the waste places of the wilderness and creating a city on a hill were definitely seen as part of God's commandment to the Massachusetts Bay colonists. Good Christian work it was believed would not go unrewarded. The Reverend William Corbin promised his people that it would "cause the Heavens to drop Fatness round about your Habitations, and the Earth to bring forth Plenty; and you shall not fail of abundance of all things for the maintenance of your Grandeur and comfort of your Lives . . ."[2] And many substantial New Englanders found that the promises were fulfilled. As it was said of the Quakers in Pennsylvania, they came to do good and did well. Nevertheless the tension between the two motives was maintained in principle as the following set of admonitions from Cotton Mather's sermon "A Christian at his Calling" indicates:

A Christian should with PIETY follow his *Occupation*. . . . Oh, let every Christian *Walk* with *God*, when he *Works* at his *Calling*, and Act in his *Occupation* with an Eye to *God*, Act as under the Eye of *God*. Syrs, 'Tis a wondrous thing that I am going to say! A poor man, that minds the *Business* of his Calling, and weaves a Threed of *Holines* into all his *Business*, may arrive to some of the highest Glories in Heaven at the last. . . .

But now, these things call for your Attention.

First; Let not the *Business* of your *Personal Calling* swallow up the *Business* of your GENERAL CALLING. Man, Be jealous lest the Fate of *Corah's* Company be thy Fate; even to be *Swallowed up of the Earth*. . . . Forget not, O *Mortal man*, That thou hast an *Immortal Soul* to be provided for. Let not that care, *What shall I Eat or Drink, and wherewithal shall I be Clothed?* make you forgetful of that care, *What shall I do to be Saved?* It may be said to many a man, who is drown'd in the Encumbrances of his Occupation; as Luk. 10.41,42. *Thou art careful and troubled about many Things; But one thing is Needful.* Thus, thou art careful to do the *Business,* that must be done for the Relief of thy *Bodily Wants;* It is well: Do it, Do it. But, thy *Soul,* thy *Soul,* the Salvation of thy *Soul,* an Acquaintance with *Christ* and an Union with *Christ,* the only Saviour of thy *Soul;* This is the ONE THING that is *Needful.* Be not so *Foolish* and *Unwise,* as to Neglect *That,* whatever thou doest! Oh, try and see if you don't upon trial find, besides the vast *Blessings of Eternity,* the Fulfilment of that word, Mat. 6.33. *Seek first the Kingdom of God, & all these things shall be added unto you.*[3]

John Bunyan's *Pilgrim's Progress* provided one of the most influential patterns of the Christian life in American history. The book was already a best seller in 17th-century New England and continued to hold a place second only to the Bible in pious American families for many decades. It was widely read down through the 19th and even into the 20th centuries. It is the story of Christian who, entering the way of salvation through the straight and narrow wicket of Christ, who relieves him of his burden of sin, proceeds to pass through the temptations and persecutions of the world until finally reaching the Heavenly City. For Mather excessive attention to the business of our personal calling or our bodily wants were just such temptations diverting us from the Way leading to the Heavenly City even though in their own subordinate place such things are not wrong.

3

It has become fashionable to argue that the Puritans were not puritanical, that they had a naturalistic view of the body, accepted its natural functioning, and could talk about it without the hushed prudery of the Victorians. That may be true, but the Puritans still had a profound suspicion of the body, a suspicion that has by no means ceased to operate in American culture, and felt that of all things creaturely it was most "prone to degeneration and extraordinarily susceptible to corruption." The adjectives they commonly applied to it were "vile," "filthy," and "unclean." Jonathan Mitchell epitomized the Puritan view when he called it "the old Crazy Rotten house of the body."[4] And of the various corruptions to which the body was prone the sexual was undoubtedly the one most emphasized. To understand the Puritan suspicion of sex and the body we must ask about its broader meaning in the great economy of the relation of God and man. The body and especially sex were dangerous because they had the power to pull man away from his dependence on God and make him find his principle in himself. To the Calvinists the condition of man is total depravity. He can do nothing without the grace of God. To imagine that one can accomplish one's own salvation is evident proof of one's damnation. As Cotton Mather said, "They *trust in their own Hearts,* and they are *Fools.*"[5] The body is feared then not for itself but because it is the source of rebellion against God. Blinded by our lusts we fail to see the divine plan for our own salvation, and so, blinded, we go to our eternal doom.

There was, nonetheless, a preoccupation with a few symbolic sins that must strike the modern observer as nearly pathological, and we will see in the next chapter how such preoccupations could lead to aggression against others. When Mather established his "Society to Suppress Disorders" the chief "Disorders" to be suppressed were drunkenness, profanity, and fornication.[6] Members of the society were to observe instances of such behavior and report to the group. When one of the members of the society collected a list of young men who frequented whorehouses in Boston, Mather set the so-

ciety to "writing reproving letters to each of the fornica-
tors."[7] But if these particular strayings from the straight
and narrow path seem to have taken up an inordinate
amount of the energy of Mather and his colleagues, they
were aware of and frequently reproved the deeper social
sins of absorption in the pursuit of private gain and lack
of charity to one's brothers. With classic terminology but
with an emotional insistence not common in the earlier
generations of New England Puritans, Cotton Mather
preached that the only hope of reform from these various forms of wickedness was to be born again in Christ,
to rise again, not with one's own strength but with his.[8]
As Mather began to despair that any general reformation
of this sort would occur—it would not until Jonathan
Edwards' Great Awakening of 1740, 12 years after Cotton Mather's death—he dwelt more and more on
prophecies of the end of times. If this generation is sunk
in its own wickedness, he thought, perhaps God will soon
act to bring about a new heaven and a new earth, to effect
drastically the reform that Mather could not bring about
by his own preaching. With his succession of rejected
schemes for the improvement of his fellows, with his
deep suspicion of his own motives and those of others,
with an increasingly unbalanced third wife shouting violent imprecations on him, Cotton Mather in his last years
is a tragic figure. But unlike so many in the generations
to follow, he knew who he was, why he was here and
where he was going. That precious cup of meaning,
which has been draining away in America ever since, was,
for him, still full.

4

If, for our purposes, Cotton Mather can stand as a kind
of archetype of Puritanism, with his very considerable
impulsive energy kept in tight control and consecrated

with meaning by its service to the divine plan, Benjamin Franklin may serve, as he has for so many others, as an archetype of the worldly American. Actually the distance between the two men was in some ways not very great. Though he satirized Mather in an early piece, Franklin was deeply influenced by Mather's "Essays To Do Good"; they provided the scaffolding for his own philosophy. Furthermore Franklin's first reading was *Pilgrim's Progress* and Bunyan was his favorite author. Charles Sanford argues persuasively that Franklin's famous *Autobiography* was indeed modeled on *Pilgrim's Progress.* It was a story of Franklin's trials and tribulations on the road to worldly success parallel to Christian's trials and tribulations on the road to the Heavenly City.[9] Franklin's scheme of moral perfection, though Mather would have abhorred it as a work of the self entirely devoid of grace, was clearly Puritan in content.

And yet, though every element is familiarly Puritan, the pattern in the kaleidoscope has altered radically and we are clearly in a different world from that of Cotton Mather. Mather's divine plan has not disappeared but it has become thin, abstract, and attenuated. There is no biblical God but there is still a deistic Supreme Being. There is no Last Judgment but there is still an afterlife where good will be rewarded and evil punished. But there is no conversion, no rebirth in Christ, and no covenant. Instead there is the pursuit of private secular advancement and public secular good without any concern such as Mather would have shown, as to how much the latter was really a form of the former. Piety has been replaced by prudence. And yet for all that enormous change, the balance between impulse and control has scarcely altered. That is what drove D. H. Lawrence to a frenzy in his chapter on Franklin where he tears the *Autobiography* apart to display the anatomy of the essential American. Franklin may allow himself a few more slips or a little less guilt about the slips than Mather did, but what Lawrence called the "barbed-wire of shalt-not ideals" is still up.[10] Though now we cannot tell for sure whether virtue is pursued for its own good or for the public seeming of good ("Honesty is the best policy" clearly illustrates the problem) the impulse life is still tightly reined in. Perhaps it is even more diminished, for the ends to which the impulses are controlled are so much less heroic and intense than were Mather's.

We should not forget, of course, that Franklin was far from devoted to mere private gain. He was one of the great actors of the Revolution and he genuinely participated in the dialectic of liberation and the constitution of liberty there enacted. But in the end, the atmosphere of the Boston apprentice who made good in Philadelphia overcomes the noble stance of the Founding Father, and we remember his calculated prudence far better than his republican virtue. Yet for all his worldliness compared to Mather—and it would be hard to imagine Mather more out of his depth than he would have been had he tried to take Franklin's place at the court of Versailles—Franklin has a kind of moral innocence that Mather did not share. Lawrence says that there is in Franklin something of a child or of an old man, or of a child wiser than its grandfather. But there is not the moral complexity of adult experience. There is an emotional and imaginative constriction about Franklin that is again essentially American, and because of it he seems somehow to escape the ravages of guilt and despair, and he never cries "What must I do to be saved?" He is the first of a long and illustrious line of American once-born men—men with no deep need for spiritual rebirth—devoted indistinguishably to themselves and their duties, childishly pleased with their own success, and only very occasionally tasting the bitter savor of ashes.

5

It would not be at all correct to assume that the transition from Cotton Mather to Benjamin Franklin is some kind of shift from the religious to the secular irreversibly accomplished once and for all. We should remember that Jonathan Edwards, a hero of piety who far outshone Mather and a quintessential twice-born man, was almost Franklin's exact contemporary, being only three years older, and would exert an influence that, if less spectacular, was no less persistent than Franklin's to the present day. And Franklin's *Autobiography,* though modeled after *Pilgrim's Progress,* did not replace it. Indeed generations of Americans would read both books, feel the pull of both images of the path of life, and not always be able to distinguish very clearly between them.

And yet it is also true that Jonathan Edwards was the last Protestant theologian before the 20th century to have in his control the entire imaginative resources of the Christian tradition.[11] Edwards's use of imagery was unparalleled and he stood at the beginning of the American tradition of revivalist preaching. He was also at home in the architectonic structure of Christian thought, the system of implications of the Christian myth. After him such a union of persuasion and thought tends to fall apart. There were vivid preachers by the score and dry as dust systematic theologians by the dozen, but there was no American again who was sufficiently at home with the structure of Christian symbolism to mold it creatively to present need until quite recently, when new impulses from secular culture and European thought have opened up new possibilities.

I do not pretend to understand all the reasons for this gradual drying up of the Protestant imagination in America—and the failure of creativity at the symbolic level should not blind us to the continuing power of the

Protestant impulse in personal character and social movements. But surely one cause that cannot be overlooked was the growing dominance in America from the middle of the 18th century of what William Blake called "single vision," and the entire social and cultural complex that went with it. Single vision was that view of the world, propagated by what Blake saw as the infernal trio —Bacon and Newton and Locke—which depended on reason alone and felt no need of the imaginative vision long nurtured in the religious and poetic traditions of the West. Twofold vision for Blake is the awareness that there is always more than what appears, that behind every evident literal fact is an unfathomable depth of implication and meaning. And Blake, who thought much about America and whose insights are deeply relevant to the American experience—though it took a century for Americans to discover him—believed that the cutting off of that depth of meaning, which for him, is what single vision does, is a kind of sleep or death. When we remember that Jefferson's three intellectual heros were Bacon and Newton and Locke, and that Jefferson was, like most of the Founding Fathers, a once-born man, we will begin to understand the growing prevalence of single vision in the early decades of the republic. The great religious revivals of the first half of the 19th century preached a twice-born religion and converted a higher percentage of the population than in any other country. But because they led to no rebirth of twofold vision, no new mythic or symbolic creation, they could not stem the tide of single vision nor, in the end, halt the erosion of twice-born religion.

Of course we cannot account for the drying up of the Protestant imagination or the rise of single vision solely in terms of the persuasiveness of the practical utilitarianism, the unconscious Lockianism, that was so appealing to American common sense. Nor can we account for it entirely in terms of the rising prestige of experimental science that the names Bacon and Newton symbolized, important though this was. The fundamental appeal of the practical rationalism that was the grassroots basis for pragmatism, the most American of philosophies, was its fit with an expansive commercial and industrial economy and the technical advances needed to exploit the wealth of a virgin continent. The tension between building the city set on a hill and the land fever noted by Increase Mather had not diminished by the time of the Revolution. Many of the lawgivers of the republic, the framers of the Constitution, were large-scale land speculators. Neither Franklin nor Jefferson were averse to extending their property, though the latter was aware of the dangers inherent in putting money-making ahead of civic virtue. Both Franklin and Jefferson were deeply interested in scientific and technical advances that could be of benefit to the American farmer and artisan. Much that is most characteristically American—our flair for mechanics, our dynamism, our urge to build—has its context in this long experience of economic and technical growth.

But the price of concentrating so heavily on the realm of worldly practical achievement was a thinning out of other dimensions of human experience. The end result, which was not evident until the late decades of the 19th century and the early decades of the 20th, was a conception of the meaning of human life, summed up in the word "success," so narrow that Franklin and Jefferson seem giants of complexity in comparison. For with the dominance of industrial capitalism after the Civil War, success in America became a singularly literal goal—it meant success in business, or more crassly, money. As John C. Van Dyke said in 1908, "Every one knows that success with the great masses spells money."[12]

6

For the man of twofold vision nothing could be more illusory than the goal of success, nothing more false than money, and a long line of Protestant preachers in the 19th century continued to say so, though, by the end of the century some of their voices began to quaver.

In 1830 George Cookman addressed the Methodists and said that the most formidable adversaries of Christianity were "your cool, prudent, calculating, common sense men, who would reduce the question to a mere sale of profit and loss." And in 1857 Joseph Thompson said, "Commerce cannot be entrusted with the moral interests of mankind. She has no principle that can withstand a strong temptation to her insatiable cupidity."[13] And even Josiah Strong, in the 1885 book already quoted about the Anglo-Saxonizing of mankind, had a moment or two of doubt whether every characteristic of those very Anglo-Saxons whom he celebrated was compatible with Christianity. He wrote:

The tendency of human nature, intensified by our commercial activity, is to make the life a whirlpool—a great maelstrom which draws everything into itself. What is needed to-day is a grand reversal of the movement, a transformation of the life into a fountain. And in an exceptional degree is this the need of Anglo-Saxons. Their strong love of liberty, and their acquisitiveness, afford a powerful temptation to offer some substitute for self-abnegation. We would call no man master; we must take Christ as master. We would possess all things; we must surrender all things.[14]

But for many of the most widely known of the 19th-century preachers admonitions of the dangers of wealth became ever more perfunctory. Religion and wealth, religion and business, were seen more and more as part of a single enterprise. Matthew H. Smith wrote in 1854, "Adam was created and placed in the Garden of Eden for business purposes; it would have been better for the race if he had attended closely to the occupation for which he was made."[15] The great Puritans—Winthrop, Mather, Edwards—much as they emphasized the value of hard work, were deeply sensitive to the tension between religion and the world, between God and Mammon. But in the late 19th century the tension in many quarters was almost gone. D. S. Gregory, in an ethics textbook widely used in the 1880s, was able to write: "By the proper use of wealth man may greatly elevate and extend his moral work. . . . The Moral Governor has placed the power of acquisitiveness in man for a good and noble purpose. . . ."[16] And finally, in 1901 William Lawrence, Episcopal Bishop of Massachusetts, wrote:

In the long run, it is only to the man of morality that wealth comes. We believe in the harmony of God's Universe. We know that it is only by working along His laws natural and spiritual that we can work with efficiency. Only by working along the lines of right thinking and right living can the secrets and wealth of nature be revealed. . . . Godliness is in league with riches. . . . Material prosperity is helping to make the national character sweeter, more joyous, more unselfish, more Christlike. That is my answer to the question as to the relation of material prosperity to morality.[17]

Clearly in such a harmonious universe there is no need for twofold vision. Single vision reveals a single truth in religion and business. As Arminian doctrine or Arminian attitudes spread among many of the popular revivalists, the stress was on a change of will rather than a radical rebirth, on man's capacity to reform himself rather than the need for death to self and new birth in Christ. Such teachings turned the Calvinist view of the sinful nature of man almost into its opposite. Both man and the world, at least in America, are essentially innocent. There are pitfalls and temptations to be avoided but they are incidental rather than of the essence of the human condition. And in this simple and harmonious view of human existence wordly success is clear evidence of moral virtue and religious salvation. The last cultural barriers to the glorification of business success as the chief end of man were just about down by the end of the 19th century. But just as in the case of Benjamin Franklin this new and more innocent view of man did not lead to a liberation of the impulse life. If drunkenness, fornication, and so forth, no longer seemed quite so hellish as they did a century before, they were still to be avoided as impediments to business success. The emotional and imaginative constriction of the American personality in a world of common sense and plain fact became ever more evident and ever more painful to that minority of Americans who sought a larger human ideal.

7

It was Anglo-Saxon Protestants who created the gospel of wealth and the ideal of success. From that group, even as late as 1900, came over 90 percent of the men of great wealth in the society. But the gospel of wealth was disseminated to the millions, including the millions of immigrants who were seldom Anglo-Saxon or Protestant. As Ralph Gabriel has said, "This faith and philosophy became the most persuasive siren in American life. It filled the highways with farm boys trekking to the city. It drained the towns and countryside of Europe." But in the 20th century, as is always the case in America, prophets have arisen to point out the hellish side of this national ideal. Even Jonathan Edwards would have admired their rhetoric, though in the 20th century they seldom came from the church. Henry Miller has exposed the almost maniacal quality of the quest for success. In the 1920s Miller worked as personnel manager for the telegraph company in New York City and his main job was the hiring of telegraph messengers. One day the vice-president was bawling him out and said he would like to see someone write a sort of Horatio Alger book about the messengers. Of this event Miller writes:

I thought to myself—you poor old futzer, you, just wait until I get it off my chest . . . I'll give you an Horatio Alger book. . . . My head was in a whirl to leave his office. I saw the army of men, women and children that had passed through my hands, saw them weeping, begging, beseeching, imploring, cursing, spitting, fuming, threatening. I saw the tracks they left on the highways, lying on the floor of freight trains, the parents in rags, the coal box empty, the sink running over, the walls sweating and between the cold beads of sweat the cockroaches running like mad; I saw them hobbling along like twisted gnomes or falling backwards in the epileptic frenzy. . . . I saw the walls giving way and the pest pouring out like a winged fluid, and the men higher up with their iron-clad logic, waiting for it to blow over, waiting for everything to be patched up, waiting, waiting contentedly . . . saying that things were temporarily out of order. I saw the Horatio Alger hero, the dream of a sick America, mounting higher and higher, first messenger, then operator, then manager, then chief, then superintendent, then vice-president, then president, then trust magnate, then beer baron, then Lord of all the Americas, the money god, the god of gods, the clay of clay, nullity on high, zero with ninety seven thousand decimals for and aft. . . . I will give you Horatio Alger as he looks the day after the Apocalypse, when all the stink has cleared away.[18]

More recently James Baldwin described the effect of the dream of success on that one group of Americans who have been most systematically prevented from ever realizing it:

Now I think there is a very good reason why the Negro in this country has been treated for such a long time in such a cruel way, and some of the reasons are economic and some of them are political. . . . Some of them are social, and these reasons are somewhat more important because they have to do with our social panic, with our fear of losing status. This really amounts sometimes to a kind of social paranoia. One cannot afford to lose status on this peculiar kind of ladder, for the prevailing notion of American life seems to involve a kind of rung-by-rung ascension to some hideously desirable state. If this is one's concept of life, obviously one cannot afford to slip back one rung. When one slips, one slips back not a rung but back into chaos and no longer knows who he is. And this reason, this fear, suggests to me one of the real reasons for the status of the Negro in this country. In a way, the Negro tells us where the bottom is: *because he is there,* and *where* he is, beneath us, we know where the limits are and how far we must not fall. We must not fall beneath him. We must never allow ourselves to fall that low, and I am not trying to be cynical or sardonic. I think if one examines the myths which have proliferated in this country concerning the Negro, one discovers beneath these myths a kind of sleeping terror of some condition which we refuse to imagine. In a way, if the Negro were not there, we might be forced to deal within ourselves and our own personalities, with all those vices, all those conundrums, and all those mysteries with which we have invested the Negro race.[19]

8

It has been argued that the quest for success has become more modest in the 20th century, after the great concentrations of economic power have made the more sensational kinds of upward mobility less likely, and especially after the great depression. Certainly in the adolescent boys that Erik Erikson studied in the late

1940s and whom he took as in some sense typical of the American character, the success ideal seems peculiarly muted. The outstanding characteristics of these tall, slim, muscular boys, mostly Anglo-Saxon and, in Erikson's words, "mildly Protestant,"[20] were autonomy, efficiency, and decency. They had personalities well-geared to enter the American occupational sphere and attain a modest success. Autonomous, efficient, and decent young men are obviously not something any society needs to apologize for. The enormous productive achievements of just such men have made America the richest and most powerful nation in the world.

And yet Erikson noticed certain things about these young men that worried him. They avoided neurotic conflict by a certain emotional self-restriction: they did not want to talk or think too much but felt more comfortable in action, in sports or work. Indeed Erikson says, "Our boy is anti-intellectual. Anybody who thinks or feels too much seems 'queer' to him. This objection to feeling and thinking is, to some extent derived from an early mistrust of sensuality."[21] The mistrust of sensuality comes largely from experience of a mother who was apt to be somewhat frigid and moralistic, and who deliberately under-gratified him or under-mothered him as an infant. His father too, though friendly and not a threat was shy and remote and there was no intimacy with him. Such boys, Erikson found, though healthy and outgoing, were somewhat alienated from their bodies, found it hard to believe that their genitals were really part of themselves. And what worried Erikson the most and seems today the most ironic, was that these young men seemed incapable of rebellion, incapable of questioning anything basic about their own society. He could not know then that he was witnessing perhaps the last generation of all-American boys.

It is clear from the above description that though we

have come a long way from Cotton Mather, the under-
ground connections are still very strong. Perhaps we
might celebrate Erikson's typical American youth as a
rapidly vanishing type with great accomplishments in
his past. But it might be more instructive to consider
what it cost to create him. One of the costs involves the
role of women in American life. American women have
been required to play a special kind of auxiliary role.
Somehow women in the Protestant tradition have come
almost to replace the clergyman as the guardian of the
American conscience. In the 19th-century romantic
novel it was the virtuous—and, let us admit it, rather
frigid—blond-haired beauty that the hero married after
some careless adventures with a dark-haired, often non-
Anglo-Saxon temptress. The Western movie continues
the stereotype split between the good woman whom
one marries and the bar-girl whom one doesn't. It was
one of the chief functions of the good woman not only
to uphold a moral ideal for her husband but to effectively starve her son emotionally so that he would be
diverted from any temptations toward sensuality into
the proper course of decency and efficiency. The strong
silent pioneer woman who looked on stoically as her
husband and son went into action had at least the satisfaction of being the moral center of her little world
even though she was not only the source, but the chief
victim of its emotional starvation. The guilt this woman
was able to generate in her men should not be underes-
timated. It was the guilt that, more than all the coal or
electricity or even atomic power, turned the huge and
countless wheels of American industry. But the woman,
with some remarkable exceptions, was kept too busy in
her role as prime producer of the chief energy supply
in American society, male motivation, to have time to
play a role herself on the public stage. Therefore we

have many heroes but few heroines—though that, too, is changing.

I think this same syndrome helps us understand the cult of youth in American society. The American ideal, as it increasingly came to be stated in the 19th century as a tensionless harmony of moral and religious idealism and the quest for economic success, required a peculiarly innocent conception of human life. In order to keep this harmonious ideal intact Americans have had to brush aside the darker moral ambiguities of life, the tragic dimension of human existence, and maintain stalwart optimism and "positive thinking." But the middle years of life treat no man kindly and forever sow the seeds of cynicism and despair. For the last century or more, one of the great tactics for keeping the ideal of shining innocence alive even in later years is to concentrate it on the young. Thoreau said, "Every child begins the world again." The sense that each young man is a new unfallen Adam is deep in 19th-century American consciousness, abhorrent as this is to religious orthodoxy. But what a burden the idolization of golden youth has always placed on the young! For it is not youth as such but our ideal of youth that we demand in them. To save our fading illusions and defend us from our deepening cynicism they must be trim, fair-haired, clean in mind and body, ambitious. (I am reminded of the injunction of the American missionary to Japan whose words, "Boys, be ambitious," is the motto of Hokkaido University, a worthy gift from one nation of compulsive achievers to another.) In other words they must be all that we want to be and fear we are not. And generation after generation with only an occasional murmur, youth did what they were bidden to do, took up the burden of guilt, and tried to realize the ideals that the fathers had failed to attain.

I wonder how many of the thousands of commencement speakers, who have over the years magnanimously informed the graduating class that it is now up to them to solve the problems of the world, have realized that they included the implicit proviso: to solve those problems according to our ideals and our methods, to succeed where we have failed, to take the weight of guilt that we can no longer bear. It seems to me that one of the many things this present generation means to say by its appearance and actions is, "No, we are not clean-cut, we are not ambitious, we are not even good as you mean good, and we will not take your burden of guilt and we will not solve your problems the way you want them solved, and we will not protect you from your fears nor bolster your illusions." But this generation too is still deeply American, in both the best and the worst meaning of the word.

We have seen how the American success ideal has taken its toll on women, on youth, on all groups who do not approximate the Anglo-Saxon Protestant ideal of character—above all on blacks. I have heard it said by some of our younger radicals that the real oppressors in American society and the only beneficiaries of the American system are the white, male, Anglo-Saxon Protestants. It is true that many of the chief rewards of the system do go to such men, and many of them seem to derive great satisfaction from them. Of course one should not forget the millions of poor whites, not only in Appalachia but in the city slums, who are Anglo-Saxon and Protestant and get few rewards of any kind. But even within the more favored section of that group, what of the white Anglo-Saxon boy who thinks or feels too much, who hears a different drummer, or sees a different vision? We should not forget the history of those who tried to revive the life of the imagination in America after life began to drain out of the Protestant Churches; how America virtually ignored a Thoreau, a Melville, and a Whitman during their lifetimes; how Poe was driven insane, Henry James into exile, and Hart Crane into suicide. (The problem for creative women was, if anything, worse. Think of Emily Dickinson.) And if those names seem somehow too atypical and it is said that genius has a difficult time in any society, then we should remember the "lives of quiet desperation" of the successful or almost successful, the double martinis that become triple martinis in the effort to wash out the taste of ashes, as well as the despair of those who have failed in their effort to climb the barbaric ladder.

All of these considerations do not change the fact that for a long time American society has been organized around the image of the successful white Anglo-Saxon man, nor assuage the bitterness of those excluded from the central rewards of the society because of the fact of sex or race or age.[22] Plato long ago pointed out that the tyrant who can gratify every whim is the greatest slave of all, because he is completely at the mercy of his own desires, but he did not mean that argument as an excuse for tyrants. There is no point in overlooking the price that white male Americans have paid for their rewards, for they have much to contribute and much to gain from a conception of the meaning of life different from the late American preoccupation with success. But the rewards, tarnished though they are, must begin to be shared more widely now.

9

Let me return to our central theme, the dialectic between liberation and liberty, revolution and constitution, conversion and covenant. In the pattern of individual life this dialectic takes the form of impulse and control. We have seen how what began as the great Puritan cosmic drama of sin and salvation, conversion, new birth and new life, became domesticated into the production of just the right amount of autonomy and guilt, decency, and efficiency to run a vast industrial economy. One of the distinctive issues of the third time of trial that we have now entered is that the existing balance in this sphere is being questioned. The question is being asked whether the price for the present pattern is not too high, whether we could not, without losing the many good things in our society, have a freer impulse life, a richer imaginative consciousness, be less alienated from our bodies, be capable of more profound intimacy with a few and more community with many others. It is also being asked whether women and youth and minority groups and even white men have to play just the roles they have been assigned in the past in order to maintain just the right balance of energy and repression in an industrial society.

The issues are vexed, and we will be returning to them in the last chapter. But a few things are sufficiently clear to say now. To those who say the answer to our present need is no control at all, let the impulses run free, natural man is at heart innocent and good, I would with Melville reply: "Well, well, one hears the kettledrums of hell." The great antinomies of human life are never solved by grasping one polarity and forgetting the other. Our problem is not to get rid of control in any absolute sense but to find a new kind of control that will allow a wider freedom. It is hard for this generation to understand a phrase like "those wise restraints that make men free," perhaps because such phrases too often have been used as part of a con game to get youth to buy the illusions of middle age. But short of the Apocalypse, there is no freedom without constraint. The great urge at the moment, and rightly so in my opinion, is liberation. But without a new order, without a new system of control, liberation cannot become liberty and quickly becomes despotism. As when some superliberated youth jumps into the arms of a totalitarian religious or political sect.

With respect to the human personality, the deepest ordering of impulse is cultural, is religious, occurs in myth and ritual. America began when the great new mythic ordering of the Protestant Reformation was still vital and alive. That pattern combined with the newer myth of republican liberty sustained and reinvigorated us in our first and second times of trial. But now our cultural crisis is deeper. The single vision that has been on the rise since the 18th century is now more than ever the dominant cultural orientation. A profound experience of conversion, of the reordering of the deepest levels of the personality in the light of a transcendent vision, is not absent in America, but it is harder than ever to integrate with the dominant cultural mood. The established structures of economic and political power seem perversely set on maximizing wealth and power regardless of the cost to the society or the natural environment. Under these circumstances we should not be surprised if efforts at liberation, revolution, and counterculture seem fragmented and chaotic. Anarchy and antinomianism are always present in the effort to change a social order that has become too constricting.

But the dominant American cultural and social system can put up with a certain amount of anarchy and antinomianism, can even encourage it. A highly private "freedom" in certain restricted spheres can go together with the dominance of purely technical control at the center of social power. From this point of view the mere rejection of the established order, even if flamboyantly symbolized, has a strictly limited utility. If we are to transcend the limitations of American culture and society it can only be on the basis of an imaginative vision that can generate an experience of inner conversion and lead to a new form of covenant. Liberation without any sense of constitution will surely be self-defeating. The perils of late 20th-century America will not be overcome by everyone doing his or her "own thing," but through the discovery of cultural and social forms that can give the disciplined basis for a new degree of moral freedom.

IV

Nativism and Cultural Pluralism in America

IN THE last chapter we considered the place of the individual in the developing pattern of symbol and myth in America. Now, in that same pattern, we must consider the place of the group, particularly groups that differed significantly from the majority of the early colonists.

In 1614 the Reverend Samuel Purchas, one of the first Englishmen to describe the new world opened up by the great explorations, wrote the following panegyric to the unity of mankind religiously conceived:

... the tawney Moore, blacke Negro, duskie Libyan, ash-coloured Indian, olive-coloured American, should with the whiter European become *one sheep-fold,* under *one great Sheep-heard,* till this *mortalitie being swallowed up of Life,* wee may all *be one, as he and the father are one* ... without any more distinction of Colour, Nation, Language, Sexe, Condition, all may bee *One* in him that is One, and *onely blessed for ever.*[1]

Five years later, the first group of Negro slaves was landed at Jamestown, Virginia. In 17th-century America the commonest way to make the distinction between white and black was to speak of Christians and Negroes. On the one hand being a Christian meant a deep commitment to the oneness of man; on the other it meant the right of Christian Europeans to enslave or destroy any who differed radically from them in belief, custom, and complexion. The dialectic between universalism and particularism, between inclusion and exclusion is found among all peoples. But nowhere more than in America has a universal conception of man existed side by side with such harsh and brutal exclusions.

The problem of inclusion and exclusion has been especially acute with respect to racial groups but it has also arisen in connection with the national, linguistic, and ethnic groups who have come as immigrants to these shores. All Americans except the Indians are immigrants or the descendents of immigrants, but not all immigrants have met the same reception. The way various groups have been treated and the place they have found in the national community is a critical index of how far American values have been realized in practice, how far our pretension to be a universal community has become actual. The struggle of oppressed racial groups to improve their position in America is a major aspect of our third time of trial. That struggle has called into question all the existing beliefs about America as a successful multicultural nation. We will have to consider both the idea and the reality of cultural pluralism to see whether it has any substance or is merely a screen for the dominance of the Anglo-Saxon minority.

America as an asylum for the oppressed is one of the oldest elements of the national myth, part of the millennial meaning of the American experiment. The Jewish American poet, Emma Lazarus, gave classic expression to this idea in 1883 in words inscribed on the pedestal of the Statue of Liberty:

> Give me your tired, your poor,
> Your huddled masses yearning to breathe free,
> The wretched refuse of your teeming shore,
> Send these, the homeless, tempest-tost to me,
> I lift my lamp beside the golden door![2]

The image of America the openhearted, receiving the afflicted of the world, has deep historical and emotional roots. Emerson, Melville, and Whitman all celebrated the variety of nations coming to these shores and intermingling to form a new people. In 1817 Jefferson saw America's open door to the oppressed as part of her meaning to the world. It was her role, he said, "to consecrate a sanctuary for those whom the misrule of Europe may compel to seek happiness in other climes. This refuge once known will produce reaction on the happiness even of those who remain there, by warning their taskmasters that when the evils of Egyptian oppression became heavier than those of the abandonment of country, another Canaan is open where their subjects will be received as brothers and secured against like oppression by a participation in the right of self-government."[3] Even before the establishment of the republic the British colonies had something of the same role which Benjamin Franklin described in 1752 in *Poor Richard Improved* as follows:

> Where the sick Stranger joys to find a Home,
> Where casual Ill, maimed Labour, freely come;
> Those worn with Age, Infirmity or Care,
> Find Rest, Relief, and Health returning fair.[4]

But it is also in Franklin that we find one of the first complaints about immigrants. He expresses the anxiety and hostility that immigrants would meet all through subsequent American history. Franklin complained of the German immigrants to Pennsylvania, whom he refers to as Dutch:

This will in a few years become a German Colony: Instead of their Learning our Language, we must learn their's, or live as in a foreign country. Already the English begin to quit particular Neighbourhoods surrounded by Dutch, being made uneasy by the Disagreeableness of Dissonant Manners; and in Time, Numbers will probably quit the Province for the same Reason. Besides, the Dutch under-live, and are thereby enabled to under-work and under-sell the English; who are thereby extremely incommoded, and consequently disgusted, so that there can be no cordial Affection or Unity between the two Nations.[5]

Implicit in Franklin's remarks is the assumption that if the Germans would only give up their "foreign language," their "dissonant manners," and their proclivity to undercut native Americans in the labor market and in trade, all would go well. Thus Franklin seems to be propounding a very early form of what would later be termed "Americanization." We will have to consider later what if anything in the basic republican values of the nation or even in its underlying religio-political myth justifies that proviso of "Americanization" or, as it has more recently been called, "Anglo-conformity."[6]

What "the homeless, tempest-tost" were supposed to find once they arrived on these shores was an "open society," with "equality of opportunity." In 1878 Emerson stated the cultural assumption well when he said, "Opportunity of civil rights, of education, of personal power, and not less of wealth; doors wide open . . . invitation to every nation, to every race and skin, . . . hospitality of fair field and equal laws to all. Let them compete, and success to the strongest, the wisest, and the best. The land is wide enough, the soil has bread for all."[7]

There is no need to question Emerson's sincerity, but there is need to question his empirical accuracy. No doubt for some groups and in some areas of social life there was genuinely open competition and opportunity. Compared to European societies divided by insuperable barriers of class, religious prejudice, and linguistic difference there was relatively more openness in America. And yet for many, even of those children of immigrants who would later go to Ivy League schools and wear Brooks Brothers suits, many doors remained closed. Milton Gordon puts the case very succinctly:

Those who had for a time ventured out gingerly or confidently as the case may be, had been lured by the vision of an "American" social structure that was somehow larger than all subgroups and ethnically neutral. And were they, too, not Americans? But they found to their dismay that at the primary group level a neutral American social structure was a myth—a mirage. What at a distance seemed to be a quasi-public edifice flying only the all-inclusive flag of American nationality turned out, on closer inspection, to be the clubhouse of a particular ethnic group—the white Anglo-Saxon Protestants, its operation shot through with the premises and expectations of its parental ethnicity.[8]

There are many ways in which apparently open doors may turn out to be closed. People of some ethnic backgrounds are not welcome in certain country clubs or yacht clubs, or there may be an invisible barrier in the corporate structure above which members of certain ethnic groups very seldom rise. But there is one group above all others for whom the proclaimed openness of

American society has proven false, and that is the Negro. Blacks along with other Americans have been exposed to the exalted ideal of success described in Chapter III. But for no other group has it turned out to be such a mirage. The moment that mirage is discovered has been a formative experience for many militant black leaders.

Malcolm X tells of growing up in a small Midwestern town. He had done very well in school and had received excellent grades. He was well liked by the other students and had been elected class president in the seventh grade. One day when he was about to enter high school, a teacher whom he trusted asked him if he had any thoughts of a career. Impulsively he replied that he had been thinking about being a lawyer. The teacher looked surprised and replied,

Malcolm, one of life's first needs is for us to be realistic. Don't misunderstand me now. We all here like you, you know that. But you've got to be realistic about being a nigger. A lawyer —that's no realistic goal for a nigger. You need to think about something you *can* be. You're good with your hands—making things. Everybody admires your carpentery shop work. Why don't you plan on carpentery? People like you as a person— you'd get all kinds of work.[9]

The story of W.E.B. DuBois might seem to be more fortunate but in its own way it was equally cruel. Like Malcolm X, Du Bois did extremely well in the public schools of the town of Great Barrington, Massachusetts, where he grew up. He was outstanding in all lines of activity and well liked by all. As his father left his mother when he was quite young, and his mother had quite limited means, the townspeople decided to raise money so that Du Bois could go to college. He expected to go to Harvard or Amherst as others from his community usually did, but he learned to his surprise that it had been determined to send him to Fisk University, an all-black institution in Nashville, Tennessee. It is this kind of experience, suffered in milder form by many immigrant groups, that leads Harold Cruse, perhaps the most thoughtful of contemporary black intellectuals, to write:

America is an unfinished nation—the product of a badly bungled process of inter-group cultural fusion. America is a nation that lies to itself about who and what it is. It is a nation of minorities ruled by a minority of one—it thinks and acts as if it were a nation of white Anglo-Saxon Protestants. This white Anglo-Saxon ideal, this lofty dream of a minority at the summit of its economic and political power and the height of its historical self-delusions, has led this nation to the brink of self-destruction. And on its way, it has effectively dissuaded, crippled and smothered the cultivation of a democratic cultural pluralism in America.[10]

2

In many cultural characteristics Americans of all backgrounds have become remarkably similar. Differences of class are often more marked than by ethnic group or even race. Differences in food preferences, dialect, and expressive culture remain, and differences connected with religion seem to be especially tenacious. Yet what is shared probably outweighs what is different for almost all groups except those American Indian communities that have been able to maintain their own language and native religion within the semi-isolation of the reservation. Mexican-Americans in areas of the Southwest where they are densely settled and maintain their own language are perhaps the next most distinct group.

Questions have recently been raised as to how deep the apparent assimilation has gone, whether inner qualities of feeling, ways of relating to others, conceptions of the meaning of life, have not been more resistant than has long been assumed. Even so we can ask how millions of immigrants from a variety of European and Asian nations have been turned in a generation or two, even superficially, into relatively homogeneous Americans. There certainly were elements of what might almost be called forced conversion, especially in the period of the First World War and the years immediately after. It was then that there was a fervent campaign to end "hyphenated Americans," and bring about 100 percent Americanization. A festival sponsored by Henry Ford in the early 1920s symbolizes this Americanization campaign. A giant pot was built outside the gates of his factory into which danced groups of gaily dressed immigrants singing their native songs. From the other side of the pot emerged a single stream of Americans dressed alike in the contemporary standard dress and singing the national anthem. As the tarantellas and the polkas at last faded away, only the rising strains of the Star Spangled Banner could be heard as all the immigrants emerged from the melting pot of Americanization. In the long run, of course, it was the public schools (and hardly less, the parochial schools) that transformed the second and the third generations.

Anglo-Saxons were the dominant ethnic group in America and self-conscious proponents of Americanization were apt to come from that group. Even so, Anglo-conformity is not an entirely apt phrase with which to characterize the American culture of the 20th century or even of the 19th. It was certainly a very different culture from that of Britain or even of English Canada. It was the product not only of ethnic inheritances but also of unique experiences in this country, in particular the experience of independence, of striking out on one's own, leaving the old world behind. The Anglo-Saxons were merely the first to undergo what would be the experience of every immigrant group.

3

In dealing with the relation between groups in America we may distinguish between three dimensions along which dominance can be measured: the cultural, the political, and the social. I would argue that the dominance of the Anglo-Saxon ethnic group has been by no means equal in all these dimensions. Or, perhaps better, that the Anglo-Saxon dominance has declined along all three dimensions, first in the political sphere, second in the cultural, and only quite recently has its social dominance been seriously challenged. Let us look first at the political dimension.

Analysts such as Gordon and Cruse recognize that there are central aspects of the American political system that they do not wish to define as the exclusive property of Anglo-Saxons but rather claim for all Americans. In this they are quite right, for many of these elements have long since been extricated from the matrix of Anglo-Saxon ethnic identity. The English political tradition underlies the institutions of the American republic, but the particular structures that resulted from the Revolution were not continuous with the British model. They were the product of an extensive study of traditions of republican thought and institutions from the entire history of the West. The American Revolution was part of a broad ferment in Atlantic society and was not confined to the English-speaking peoples. The influence of French political thought and continental natural-rights theories were major components of the emerging American political ideology. But leaving aside sources of influence, the crystallization of American political institutions is remarkably free of any cultural symbolization that would confine their benefits to those of Anglo-Saxon descent.

On the contrary, the American Revolution spoke, particularly in the Declaration of Independence, in the accent of mankind in general. American revolutionary thought had the capacity to transcend ethnic barriers, as its influence on revolutionary movements all over the world, from the French Revolution of 1789 to that of Ho Chi Minh in Vietnam after the Second World War shows. When W. E. B. Du Bois spoke in 1903 about embracing the "greater ideals of the American Republic" and the "spirit of the Declaration of Independence"[11] he was only doing in the language of his day what Gordon and Cruse in our own time do when they espouse democracy and pluralism as fundamental to the American republic. Though Anglo-Saxons may have formulated these ideals originally and, at least in principle, committed the society to them, they are not exclusively Anglo-Saxon ideals. Even men like Garrison, who seem to reject the proclaimed ideology of America, do so because they believe those who assert the ideals of that ideology have subverted them. The ideal of equal protection of the law for everyone in the exercise of his or her natural rights is not an ideal for Anglo-Saxons alone. Its validity and appeal remain even when it is betrayed by the very Anglo-Saxon group that originally formulated it.

That larger promise remained moot for a long time, and Anglo-Saxon dominance in the political sphere is not completely gone even today. But already by the later decades of the 19th century some immigrants, notably the Irish, were able to exercise political power at least at the local level. In the 20th century major ethnic groups and even racial groups began to be represented on the national political stage and the election of the first Catholic president in 1960 marked the crossing of an important symbolic barrier. Inadequate as the representation of certain groups may be, American political life clearly includes the active participation of many ethnic and racial groups besides the Anglo-Saxons in the late decades of the 20th century.

Turning to the cultural dimension, I would argue that American culture was moving out from under the dominance of purely Anglo-Saxon ethnic considerations even before the Revolution. The influence of the enlightenment philosophers is the crucial influence in the 18th century. Enlightenment thought not only affected specifically political institutions, it also influenced the way the religious tradition would be formulated at the level of national culture. The biblical imagery underlying the conception of the new nation was sufficiently generalized, sufficiently pruned of anything specifically Protestant, so that both Catholics and Jews could easily echo it. Rabbi Wise followed the general pattern, as we have seen. Catholic expressions of the special mission of America—in Archbishop John Ireland's words, "A chosen nation of the future!"—would often outdo their Protestant models. The use of biblical figures to express the meaning of American history was by no means an Anglo-Saxon monopoly. They have even been used to quite critical effect by black Americans.

Among the intellectuals who championed these universalistic components of the national ideology were some who were self-conscious representatives of the Anglo-Saxon ethnic group. They argued that though the ideals were universal the Anglo-Saxons were their ablest representatives and that their leadership of the world was necessary in order to "Anglo-Saxonize" mankind. But the most outstanding of the American intellectuals who began to emerge in the 19th century outside the ranks of the Protestant clergy were often sharp critics of

Anglo-Saxon pretensions. While second-rank intellectuals, often popular in their own day, were providing ideology and leadership for nativism, the major figures of classic American literature and thought were self-consciously extricating themselves from the prejudices and presuppositions of their own ethnic group rather than reflecting and glorifying them. That is one reason they were so often ignored in their own day. Especially since the First World War it is very hard to find an Anglo-Saxon intellectual of the first rank who will take a narrow ethnic-group position.

The highly critical stance of Anglo-American intellectuals to much in the outlook of their own ethnic group has had the negative result of isolating them and reducing their influence on their own group. The alienation of the intellectuals from their own religious tradition, and the loss of intellectual creativity in the Protestant Churches, that is both cause and effect of that alienation, has further weakened their influence. But their critical stance has had the consequence, as Milton Gordon has pointed out,[12] that the intellectuals are the one major group in American society that is open to individuals of all ethnic backgrounds, in practice as well as in theory. And it is among intellectuals that primary-group association and intermarriage between those of different ethnic and religious background is more the rule than the exception. A qualification has to be made, as usual, with respect to the blacks and even more to groups like the Indians and the Chicanos whose social situation has virtually prevented the emergence of intellectuals in the modern sense. But even in these cases the lack of full integration can be understood, more because of the special forms of oppression they suffer in American society than from any intrinsic closure of intellectual institutions to them. The absorption of very large numbers of Jews and significant numbers of Catholics makes it even less likely that American cultural and intellectual life, and here I am speaking of popular culture as well as high culture, will reflect an exclusively Anglo-Saxon ethnic ideal.

It is at the social level rather than the political or the cultural that America remains divided into largely self-sufficient ethnic groups. It is at the level of primary-group association—friendship, clubs, intermarriage, and to some extent neighborhood residence patterns—that ethnic exclusiveness still operates. To a considerable though declining extent, Anglo-Saxon influence is still decisive in the occupational structure and the control of economic institutions. The emergence of other ethnic groups into positions of significant power in the political and cultural systems makes it doubtful how long the Anglo-Saxons will retain even this bastion. The universalism of the political system and the relatively complete integration of the cultural elite bring into question the indefinite survival of hereditary ethnic groups in American society, or how vital they will be if they do survive. If we value cultural pluralism in America we may have to look elsewhere than to the continuation of existing ethnic groups to find a basis for such pluralism, though the persistence of ethnic and particularly religious identities cannot be entirely counted out. Here as usual we must make a partial exception for the racial groups. The emergence of ethnic pride and some degree of vitality in ethnic culture among blacks and Chicanos and the continuation of such culture among Indians fits the classical conception of cultural pluralism developed by Horace Kallen[13] better than the present condition of most of the white and oriental ethnic groups. But in these racial groups ethnic separation clearly represents a response to special oppression. There may be some pull toward generalization of the model of the racial groups but it is questionable if it will be strong enough to reverse long-standing trends away from ethnic groups as the structural location of cultural vitality in America.

4

In spite of the long-term attenuation of Anglo-Saxon cultural influence, there are continuities that link recent developments with the cultural orientations of the earliest settlers. The salvation/success polarity has tended to recur in new forms rather than to disappear. These ideals of personal fulfillment have played into the dialectic of inclusion and exclusion in the relation between ethnic and racial groups.

Among the early Puritans there was a strong sense of the difference between the saved and the reprobate, the saints and the sinners, that made any sense of community between them difficult. Robert Middlekauff summarizes the views of Increase Mather on this subject as follows:

The company a Godly man kept constituted a test of his regeneration: a truly Godly man, Increase said, delighted only in the company of other Godly men; he resented wasting his time with sinners; he did not want them to throw his mental frame out of joint. The thrust of this attitude is toward a kind of moral separation, a fear of contamination.[14]

The fear of contamination, interpreted along the lines made familiar by Freud and Durkheim, derives from the fact that the behavior of the sinners is experienced unconsciously as seductive. The inner structure of repressions supporting the character structure of the Godly man is threatened by the behavior (drunkenness, fornication, brawling) of the sinners. Increase Mather's mechanism for dealing with the threat is separation. Another is external repression of the reprobates. If sinners lack inner controls, the society can enforce outer controls on them. This logic led to Cotton Mather's societies to suppress disorders. But this effort at external control of sinners did not remain a matter for voluntary groups of saints. It affected the entire legal structure and in many respects still does. The rise of the temperance movement in the 19th century, carried by a proliferating string of voluntary associations and leading to the Eighteenth Amendment in 1919 prohibiting the manufacture, importation, and sale of alcoholic beverages, is only the most spectacular example of a mechanism that has been very widespread in American life and still exists today.

The fundamental notion of dividing society into saints and sinners, separating the saints from the sinners as much as possible, and then instituting a system of external controls to bring the sinners into at least outer conformity with the moral expectations of the saints, originally had nothing to do with the relations between ethnic and racial groups. But it was not long before certain of the characteristic traits of sinners were projected onto whole groups of people. Both Indians and Blacks were seen by the earliest Americans as prone to every kind of sinful impulse—rampant sexuality, bloodthirstiness, and sloth. When the allegedly sinful group was external to the society, the dialectic of saint and sinner could fuse with the notions of chosen people and holy war to justify extraordinary hostility and aggression against the despised group. The uncompromising ruthlessness of American warfare has seldom been orgiastic. The autonomous, decent, and efficient American described by Erikson has killed cold-bloodedly whether in fighting Indians, dropping the Atomic bomb on Japanese, or organizing search and destroy missions against the Viet Cong. It is this kind of thing that led D.H. Lawrence to say, "The essential American soul is hard, isolate, stoic, and a killer. It has never yet melted."[15] The repression of evil, regardless of the means, is a simple duty to the classic American.[16]

Where the sinful group is not external to the society but internal, stringent controls, including both rigorous policing and occasional mob violence, have long been normal in America. In the course of the 19th century, as we have seen, moral uprightness tended to become more and more defined not by religious rebirth but by secular, —especially monetary—success. And groups considered morally upright have been allowed extraordinary freedom in American society. Police and governmental controls on such groups—and they have in America always included a significant proportion of the common people as well as the upper classes—have been minimal compared to most European or Asian societies. In this respect America has indeed been remarkably voluntaristic and democratic. But such voluntarism has not been extended to groups that are deemed not to live up to established moral standards. Blacks have suffered more than any other group in American history from the projection of every rejected impulse in the unconscious white mind. They have been subjected to an unparalleled history of extreme coercion and violence which did not end with emancipation but has taken ever new forms to the present day.

But immigrant groups from the time of the first large-scale Irish immigration have also been subjected to external control and violence. The Irish were early characterized as drunken, brawling, and lazy and thus legitimate subjects for police control and mob violence. In fact American urban police forces (and public schools) emerged initially only in conjunction with large-scale immigration. Later immigrant groups, for example the

Italians, were characterized as criminal and often as sedi-
tious and further controls against them were instituted.
Of course, as such immigrant groups became accul-
turated their position with respect to such intergroup
violence and control changed. By the late 19th century
the Irish had become the archetypal American cops, just
as in the 20th century they would be the typical FBI
agents. By and large it has been only the racial groups
that have not graduated, so to speak, from the status of
controlled to the status of controller.

It was the success ideal that lured the various immigrant groups into the cultural patterns and inner controls that have gradually weakened the barriers between
them and older Americans. It would be a mistake to see
this as entirely inflicted on the immigrant groups by an
alien American culture.[17] Some form of it is what lured
many to these shores in the first place. Emma Lazarus
closed her poem with the phrase "I lift my lamp beside
the *golden* door!" What many of the immigrants hoped
for, as Hannah Arendt has pointed out, is not "to each
according to his ability," nor even "to each according to
his need" but that old dream of the poor, "to each according to his desire." That hope, in the hard conditions
of the new world, would be tamed, regulated and controlled; and more modest, more American mechanisms
of striving would be installed, if not in the immigrant at
least in his children and grandchildren. The human price
was high, for the first generation incalculably high, in
broken community and personal meaninglessness. The
American experience has always been ambiguous; never
repression alone, but also liberation; never success alone
but also, in some form or other, salvation. And so Oscar
Handlin, in his well known book *The Uprooted* can give an
answer to the unasked question of the first generation as
to what it all meant:

No longer part within some whole, you mourn the loss beyond all power of repair and, blinded, fail to see the greater gain. You may no longer now recede into the warm obscurity where like and like and like conceal the one's identity. And yet, exposed, alone, the man in you has come to life. With every hostile shock you bore, with every frantic move you made, with every lonely sacrifice, you wakened to the sense of what, long hidden in that ancient whole, you never knew you lacked. Indeed the bitter train of your misfortunes has, in unexpected measure, brought awareness of the oneness that is you; and though the separation pains now will not let you know it, the coming forth endowed you with the human birthright of your individuality.[18]

5

But no matter how we evaluate the past, and it is in many respects an ambiguous and ironic story, it is part of our third time of trial that the old verities are no longer taken for granted. While our conservatives would meet the present disorder in American society with the old formula of moralistic rhetoric and police control, others are calling into question the values and character structure that underly that very formula. For 50 years and more America's most established intellectuals, artists, and writers have been subjecting the narrower version of American character and values to devastating criticism. And they have rejected the moralistic self-righteousness, the sacrifice of all human impulses to the single goal of success, the materialism and vulgarity of so much of American life. In the last ten years or so this criticism has begun to disaffect a whole generation. Students in many American universities have begun not only to believe what many of their professors have long been saying but to act on that belief with a single-minded rigor that has often appalled their teachers. They have frequently displayed a moralistic self-righteousness and a personal vulgarity that makes one wonder whether they are criticizing American character or exemplifying it at its worst. But one must expect all kinds of pathology when a great change occurs, and the deflation of the myth of American innocence, of material success, and of the necessity to inflict aggression on various allegedly dangerous groups, is a great change indeed.

One of the more interesting features of the present situation is the transvaluation that has taken place in much of the youth culture so that the WASP is a negative image and the black, the Indian, and the Asian are culture heroes. Here too one must wonder at the depth of the change if there is too total a reversal so that we only have a new set of actors in the traditional good-guy and bad-guy roles. But some at least have begun to experiment with the logic of complementarity rather than of opposition. As long ago as his 1903 book, *The Souls of Black Folk*, W. E. B. Du Bois put forward the idea that blacks might have certain characteristics that whites desperately need. He toyed with the idea that "some day on American soil two world-races may give each to each those characteristics both so sadly lack." And he added: "We the darker ones come even now not altogether empty-handed." He cited the integrity of emotion and expression in black culture which might appear as "the sole oasis" in white culture's "dusty desert" of dollars and vulgarity.[19]

Much more recently Eldridge Cleaver has pointed out that the splitting tendency in American culture, which we have traced back to the early Puritans, tended to make the white man a mind without a body and the black man a body without a mind.[20] Only when the white man comes to respect his own body, to accept it as part of himself, will he be able to accept the black man's mind and treat him as something other than the living symbol of what he has rejected in himself. The abiding American hostility to the body and to deeper levels of the unconscious personality, was pointed out by D. H. Lawrence in 1923 and confirmed by Erik Erikson in 1950. It is part of the single vision against which classic American writers such as Melville and Whitman rebelled in the last century. Following a similar logic, Hart Crane in the 1920s found in the American Indian a symbol of the mythic consciousness that American culture had for long repressed. Recently the Indian became a symbolic focus of the counterculture.

The transvaluation of roles that turns the despised and oppressed into symbols of salvation and rebirth is nothing new in the history of human culture, but when it occurs, it is an indication of new cultural directions, perhaps of a deep cultural revolution. For it means not merely a potential change in the social position of formerly persecuted groups but a change in the balance between repression and freedom in the dominant American psyche. I do not want to imply that such changes are any more than incipient and fragile at the moment. But what is undeniable is that the defenders of the old attitudes and values have thoroughly lost confidence in themselves. If they are not ready to opt for anything radically new, they are very uncertain as to how much of the old can be or ought to be saved.

6

The changed valence given to black and Indian culture on the one hand and to WASP culture on the other raises questions about the future of cultural pluralism and community in America. One common model of the assimilation process in America saw it as a process in which immigrant groups, and eventually racial groups as well, would finally adapt themselves to an atomized and highly

mobile "rational" society that is as far from original Protestant culture as from that of any immigrant group.
Naturally, the energy for this process was to be supplied
by the continued technological and economic "development" of America. In recent years that model has come
under increasing criticism. The "mass culture" that
seems an inevitable accompaniment to industrial society
has been rejected in favor of the intimate, the personal,
the communal, the kind of culture that individuals and
small groups can make for themselves. "Community"
has become a kind of magic word. Though its use has
often been sentimental and imprecise, its prevalence is
symptomatic. Much of the new mystique of the racial
minorities comes from the fact that they are alleged to
have retained a sense of community missing among
whites. Michael Novak recently argued eloquently that
Eastern and Southern European groups have maintained
a vital sense of family and neighborhood that gives them
a different sense of reality from other Americans and that
deserves careful nurturing.[21]

Nostalgia for the rural past of Anglo-Americans, when
"community" was more of a reality than in the modern
suburbs, has even invaded the mass media of late. The
extent to which any effort to revive or even maintain
community in America without a fundamental change in
the economic system is a problem we will consider in the
next chapter. Here we can only reflect on the meaning
of the current ferment.

The rejection of the Anglo-Saxon image of the American goes very deep and there is a great effort to retrieve
the experience and history of all the repressed cultures
that "Americanization" tried to obliterate. Instead of
one American civil religion, it is argued, there are many
civil religions; instead of one covenant, many. (It is ironic
that late in its history the great Protestant word "cove-

nant" should have been used in the phrase "restrictive covenant" as a symbol of the exclusion of others.) A few critics feel that the American experiment has been so badly botched that it is even questionable that we can survive as a single society. Others look to the emergence of new collective ideals quite different from those of the past in which pluralism and community will have a prominent place.[22]

Without a great deal of research and the passage of time it is difficult to know which ethnic groups or what percentage of them will survive as separate cultural entities. For many the attrition of language, history, and custom has been so great that only a name and a label remain. We should not, however, infer from loss of cultural content to loss of actual community. As Isaac Berkson wrote over 50 years ago, "The ethnic group is not a system of ideas but a nationality, a community of persons; it is a living reality related, indeed, to thought, but still flesh and blood and desire and no mere pale abstraction."[23] Where community survives, culture can be revived. Americans may finally be ready to see that biculturalism is an advantage more than a defect and agree with Berkson that "True universalization, colloquially called 'broadmindedness,' can only come through the multiplication of loyalties, not through the supression of them. . . ."[24] The beginnings of a shift in public policy in education and other areas to the preservation of community and cultural diversity are hopeful, even though developments in this direction are still quite fragile.

The survival of ethnic identities seems to me only meaningful in the context of the survival of religious identities. Religion provides an essential mediation between the ethnic group and the larger culture of the modern world. Not only does religion often preserve the deepest symbols of ethnic identity, it also exerts a pull away from ethnic particularity to that which is morally and religiously universal. That particular ethnic groups are linked in larger religious groups, Catholic, Jewish, and Protestant, and that the religious groups share certain common symbols is undoubtedly an important element in whatever cultural unity and universality exists in America. But unfortunately not only the Protestant tradition but the Catholic and Jewish traditions have undergone severe attrition in America and in their present form it is doubtful whether they can provide the basis for a genuine cultural renewal.

The cultural vitality in America of the several religious traditions has been waning for a long time. They have been dependent on European theologians and philosophers for their inspiration. Though American Protestantism has recently produced more significant minds than at any time since the early 18th century, even the most important American theologians have had less influence here than Karl Barth or Paul Tillich. American Catholic thinkers have not rivalled Jacques Maritain or Karl Rahner, and American Jews have hardly produced figures of the magnitude of Martin Buber or Franz Rosenzweig. Even if we consider the three major religious groups as ethnic traditions rather than religious in the narrow sense, their brightest and most creative intellectuals and artists have been absorbed into the general American intellectual and artistic community so as to deprive the communal groups of their natural cultural leaders.

It is questionable whether a "return" to inherited ethnic and religious identities, at least among the more privileged white groups, would be particularly healthy. A return to primordial loyalties in the face of cultural and social breakdown can be defensive, based more on fear than joyous reaffirmation. Where the motive is the protection of one's own property and privilege against the threat of other competing groups, the political implications can be quite serious. One man's "cultural pluralism" can then become another man's "nativism," with all the classic elements of violence and repression that that entails.

Perhaps what we need, at least among the more dominant white groups, is not so much a communalism of birth as a new communalism of intention. The openness of young Protestants and Catholics to each others' traditions has never been greater and the openness of young Jews to all the religious and ideological possibilities is striking. Perhaps the revitalization of our religious traditions will come from new efforts to live them as experienced realities, rather than objects of thought, by those who find them meaningful, whatever their own origins may be. Experimentation with new cultural and social forms does not stop at the boundary of Western or biblical culture. Indian America, Africa, and above all Asia are supplying many new possible patterns. The young people flocking to Buddhist, Sufi, and Yoga groups come from all ethnic and religious backgrounds. This experimentation with symbols and ways of experiencing reality from cultures once very alien to us has even begun to influence some of the established churches. Expansive openness is as characteristic of the present situation as is the revival of the past. Perhaps, if we are to survive our third time of trial, encouragement of a broad range of experiments with cultural symbols and styles of community may be essential.

There is long precedent for such openness in American culture. R. W. B. Lewis has referred to "the unrivalled hospitality of the American imagination to the literatures of other nations. For all its occasional parochialism and its periodic bursts of cultural nativism,

American literature at its most original and adventurous is also the most international, the most cosmopolitan, the most *Western* of the literatures of the Western world."[25] I would point out that it is also unrivalled in its openness to the East, from Emerson's and Thoreau's absorption with the Bhagavad Gita to Henry Miller's Taoism and Gary Snyder's Zen Buddhism. No one has expressed American cultural openness more insistently than the archetypal American poet, Walt Whitman. In 1876, the first centennial year, he spoke of "a vaster, saner, more splendid COMRADSHIP, typifying the People everywhere, uniting closer and closer not only The American States, but all Nations, and all Humanity."[26] And in "Passage to India" he saw that the soul's travelling to distant lands is at the same time, in the twofold vision of the visionary poet, an exploration of its own depths:

Passage indeed O soul to primal thought,
Not lands and seas alone, thy own clear freshness, . . .
O soul, repressless, I with thee and thou with me,
Thy circumnavigation of the world begin,
Of man, the voyage of his mind's return,
To reason's early paradise . . .
. . . back to wisdom's birth, . . .
Again with fair creation.

But before we can explore further the possibilities of utopian renewal in contemporary America, whether we may yet recover that millennial newness that is our birthright, we first need to consider the somber reality of the American political economy. Unless its tendencies to destroy every genuine element of culture and community are brought under control, all else is in vain. The prospect does not give rise to great optimism.

V

The American Taboo on Socialism

SOCIALISM arose in Europe as a critique of industrial society early in the 19th century. A significant socialist movement exists in almost every industrial nation in the world, often going back a century or more. Socialism as an ideology is important in most of the nonindustrial nations as well. Among the major industrial nations, only America has no significant socialist movement. Although socialism was introduced to America early in its history, there is only a fragmentary socialist tradition here. The criticism of capitalism, vigorous in most industrial nations, has here been faint and fitful.

Why is it that socialism has been taboo, and capitalism sacrosanct? Is it because capitalism has "worked" in America? Is it because capitalism's beneficiaries have outnumbered its victims? Perhaps, though it has "worked" for some groups better than for others and in some periods better than in others. And it is not obvious that capitalism has worked so much better here than in many other countries where it has met a strenuous opposition. Is the apparent taboo on socialism due to the enormous repressive power of American capitalism, its power to throttle effective criticism? Again there is some truth to such an assertion. There is an old tradition of antiradical violence in America and there have been periods, such as the First World War and its immediate aftermath and the McCarthy period after the Second World War, when radical thought of all varieties has been severely persecuted. But on the whole, socialist organization has been legal in America and socialist thought uncensored. American socialists have never faced the mass arrests and the total prohibition on socialist publications that, for example, Japanese socialists have, yet socialism in Japan remains a far more vital movement than in America. The weakness of a critical socialist tradition in America cannot be explained altogether by the success of capitalism or the repression of socialism but is in part due to those features of American culture and American myth that we have been examining.[1]

2

The word "socialism" was coined in France at about the same time as the word "individualism." The two words arrived on these shores in the years between 1820 and 1840 as contrast terms for one another. In Europe individualism carried a negative implication so that socialism had, initially at least, a rather positive connotation.[2] But individualism resonated to so much that was latent in American ideology that it rapidly became the positive term. Socialism, its opposite, could only be evaluated negatively. Emerson expressed the national mood in 1847 when he said, "Individualism has never been tried," and went on to decry the vogue that socialism was enjoying just when it seemed that at last individualism might have a real chance. His position had already been worked out in 1840 when, in criticizing the communitarian experiment at Brook Farm, he said, "I do not wish to remove from my present prison to a prison a little larger. I wish to break all prisons."[3] It should be noted that Emerson was not glorifying something that already existed in America in contrast to socialism. He was certainly not glorifying capitalism, for which the name and the concept as yet scarcely existed. He was expressing his hope for the appearance of a utopian individualism that would be a fulfillment of Protestant voluntarism and Jeffersonian democracy. In a society characterized by such utopian individualism, government would be reduced to those few functions that neighbors could voluntarily agree to without infringing on the full play of individual autonomy.

It should be obvious that such a conception of individualism would not be easy to reconcile with the realities of a society dominated by industrial capitalism. Emerson was ambivalent toward the emerging symptoms of such an economic order, and Thoreau was implacably hostile to them. The ideological issue, individualism *vs.* socialism, came to a head well before industrial capitalism could even be clearly discerned in America, which was not until after the Civil War. The general rejection of socialism in America by the 1850s, after an earlier flurry of interest, is to be explained far more by the victory of the ideology of individualism than as a choice between alternate ways to order a new industrial economy whose outlines were as yet hardly discernible.

When capitalism in America did become ideologically self-conscious, it took shelter under the established categories of individualism, however incongruous that would turn out to be. In the 20th century, "free enterprise," with its connotation of early entrepreneurial capitalism easily reconciled with individualism, became the slogan of the giant corporate bureaucracy that was the reality of late American capitalism. The link between the most basic national values and the alleged characteristics of our economy are clearly spelled out in a 1946 statement by the National Association of Manufacturers in a book entitled *The American Individual Enterprise System:*

At the threshold of our national existence we solemnly asserted "the unalienable right to life, liberty, and the pursuit of happiness"; we fought the Revolutionary War for that right, and adopted a Constitution to guarantee and propagate it. We became a nation of free men not serving political masters but ourselves, free to pursue our happiness without interference from the state, with the greatest liberty of individual action ever known to man. Individuals, conscious of unbounded opportunity, inflamed by the love of achievement, inspired by the hope of profit, ambitious of the comfort, power and influence that wealth brings, turned with . . . vigor to producing and offering goods and services in freely competitive markets. The individual wanted little from the government beyond police protection while he confidently worked out his own destiny. . . . Our "private enterprise system and our American form of government are inseparable and there can be no compromise between a free economy and a governmentally dictated economy without endangering our political as well as our economic freedom."[4]

Most of the founding fathers would not have waxed quite as warm about the "hope of profit" and the ambitions for "the comfort, power and influence that wealth brings," as did the National Association of Manufacturers. But what is striking in the statement is the assertion of individual freedom against the interference of a hierarchical, bureaucratic state, while such freedom is not asserted against the interference of vast hierarchical, bureaucratic corporations, corporations that operate largely outside the normal democratic political process and are under even less popular restraint than state power.

3

In the third chapter I suggested that there is far more tension between basic American values and the capitalist economic system than is usually assumed. Much as the Puritans encouraged work in a calling, they were always aware of the dangers of making wealth and power into ends in themselves, dangers not only to one's eternal salvation but also to the coherence of the community. But in the 17th and 18th centuries, and even well into the 19th, such matters could be treated largely at the level of individual morality. With the emergence of large-scale industry in the mid-19th century the social and political implications of capitalist organization became manifest, though even today Americans tend to treat social problems as problems of personal morality. But from early times there have been a few who have shown a sharp social perception.

Already in 1781 Thomas Jefferson in his *Notes on the State of Virginia* made an analysis of the relation between economic and political life that is usually placed under the rubric of agrarianism but is considerably broader in its implication:

Those who labor in the earth are the chosen people of God, if ever he had a chosen people, whose breasts He has made His peculiar deposit for substantial and genuine virtue. It is the focus in which he keeps alive that sacred fire, which otherwise might escape from the face of the earth. Corruption of morals in the mass of cultivators is a phenomenon of which no age nor nation has furnished an example. It is the mark set on those, who, not looking up to heaven, to their own soil and industry, as does the husbandman, for their subsistence, depend for it on casualties and caprice of customers. Dependence begets subservience and venality, suffocates the germ of virtue, and prepares fit tools for the design of ambition. This, the natural progress and consequence of the arts, has sometimes perhaps been retarded by accidental circumstances; but, generally speaking, the proportion which the aggregate of the other classes of citizens bears in any State to that of its husbandmen, is the proportion of its unsound to its healthy parts and is a good enough barometer whereby to measure its degree of corruption. While we have land to labor then, let us never wish to see our citizens occupied at a work-bench, or twirling a distaff. Carpenters, masons, smiths, are wanting in husbandry; but, for the general operations of manufacture, let our work-shops remain in Europe. It is better to carry provisions and materials to workmen there, than bring them to the provisions and materials, and with them their manners and principles. The loss by the transportation of commodities across the Atlantic will be made up in happiness and permanence of government. The mobs of great cities add just so much to the support of pure government as sores do to the strength of the human body. It is the manners and spirit of a people which preserve a republic in vigor. A degeneracy in these is a canker which soon eats to the heart of its laws and constitution.[5]

There is a notable absence of the glorification of wealth, which contrasts sharply with the National Association of Manufacturers' statement. Jefferson is willing to sustain a relative poverty to gain other ends. His glorification of farmers was not based on any mystique of the soil as such. It is their independence, their lack of subservience, that sets them above merchants and artisans who are dependent on customers for their living. Jefferson believed the republic depended on the participation of autonomous individuals, each capable of making up his own mind and carrying his own responsibility. Every citizen, ideally, would be a "participator in government" and farmers were best suited to that role. By 1816, 30 years after *Notes on the State of Virginia*, Jefferson had changed his mind and concluded that manufactures were

necessary for national survival in a period of great international disturbance. But, more concerned than ever
with democratic participation, in that year he insistently
put forward his proposals for a ward system. The ward
was to be a level of government below the county that
would involve the active participation of everyone in
what he referred to as "elementary republics." He was
deeply suspicious of any system that totally delegated
political responsibility. He did not lose his original suspicion of manufacturing nor was he sanguine about the
future of democracy in America should large sectors of
the population become politically and economically dependent. In his correlative stress on individual autonomy
and genuine political community, including on its lowest
level every individual as an active participator, Jefferson
was still holding together the two sides of the American
ideal, the individual and the social, that would increasingly come apart in the century after his death.

Orestes A. Brownson, the transcendentalist Unitarian
who would later become America's leading 19th-century
Catholic thinker, was perhaps the shrewdest social analyst in the period before the Civil War. Rejecting both
utopian socialism and utopian individualism, he opted
for a balance in the tradition of American thought that
went back to John Winthrop. "Community," he said,
"without individuality is *tyranny*, the fruits of which are
oppression, degradation and immobility, the synonym of
death. Individuality without community is *individualism*,
the fruits of which are dissolution, isolation, selfishness,
disorder, anarchy, confusion, war. . . . What we need,
then is . . . communalism and individuality harmonized
. . . atoned."[6] Writing in 1840 he saw the greatest threat
to that proper balance coming not from socialism but
from capitalism. In a famous essay entitled "The Labor-
ing Classes" he depicted in stark outline what the ad-

vance of industrialism was doing to American democracy. He deplored the increasing division of Americans
into rich and poor and predicted the arrival of that "most
dreaded of all wars, the war of the poor against the
rich."[7]

Like Jefferson, Brownson argued that democratic government depends on an essential equality of social position. But the common factory laborer could never hope
to exercise the same political influence as the mill owner.
The dependency that Jefferson had deplored in merchants and artisans Brownson saw as ten times worse
among wage laborers. Brownson, writing before Karl
Marx had penned a single of his famous lines, argued
that wage labor is essentially a form of slavery. "Wages,"
he said in the 1840 article, "is a cunning device of the
devil, for the benefit of tender consciences, who would
retain all the advantages of the slave system, without the
expense, trouble, and odium of being slave-holders."[8]
He even echoed the argument that some of the Southern
apologists used for very different purposes; namely that
the slave is in some degree better off than the factory
worker since he never faces the uncertainties of unem-
ployment or the pangs of actual physical want that afflict
the latter.

Brownson's solution was thoroughly within the Jeffersonian tradition. He wished to build into the economy
conditions that would emancipate the workingman from
his wage slavery so that "by the time he is of a proper age
to settle in life, he shall have accumulated enough to be
an independent laborer on his own capital—on his own
farm or in his own shop."[9] In order to ensure the equality of opportunity ("not equal wealth, but equal chances
to wealth"[10]) that is essential in a democracy, he proposed to abolish inheritance, for he saw that without that
measure all talk of equality of opportunity is essentially

hollow. What Brownson did not see—what in 1840 was still far from obvious—was that a modern economy could not operate on the basis of small farms and shops, that it had an inherent drive toward a scale that was simply irreconcilable with the traditional American stress on every man his own master. The curious thing is that Americans have never given up that ideological commitment even when it has become almost totally remote from social and economic reality.

Walt Whitman was a far less acute social analyst than Brownson and in many of his social views reflected his environment. It is therefore interesting to find him in the 1880s saying, at the very moment that the giant corporate trusts were forming: "I look forward to a world of small owners. . . . The creation of a large, independent, democratic class of small owners is the main thing."[11] He called for the "production and perennial establishment of millions of comfortable city homesteads and moderate-sized farms, healthy and independent, single separate ownership, fee simple, life in them complete but cheap, within reach of all."[12] This, it should be noted, is not the dream of wealth, power, and influence. It is the late 19th-century version of the old Puritan republican dream of a genuine participatory democracy. And Whitman's gnawing fear was expressed in imagery almost identical with that of Jefferson: "If the United States, like the countries of the Old World, are also to grow vast crops of poor, desperate, dissatisfied, nomadic, miserably-waged populations, such as we see looming upon us of late years—steadily, even if slowly, eating into them like a cancer of lungs or stomach—then our republican experiment, notwithstanding all its surface-successes, is at heart an unhealthy failure."[13]

In spite of a long series of struggles to protect and expand the role of the independent producer in America, struggles led by loco-foco Democrats, free-soil Republicans, populists, progressives, and New Dealers, and in spite of specific legislative programs—the dismantling of the United States Bank, the Homestead Act, the antitrust laws, the federal loan programs for farmers and small businessmen—the concentration and bureaucratization of the economy has not been halted or reversed nor have the "vast crops of poor, desperate, dissatisfied, nomadic" and "miserably-waged" been diminished. The emergence of labor unionization, a degree of governmental regulation in many industries, social security, and the welfare system have kept the worst consequences of the profound disparities in the economic system, the consequences feared by Jefferson, Brownson, and Whitman, from appearing with all their potential virulence. But they have not altered the fundamental fact that the economic system of late industrial America cannot be reconciled with the fundamental American ideology of economic independence as the basis of political order. That ideology we have never abandoned though it has described our social reality less accurately with every passing decade.

4

If there is a profound disparity between the present American economic system and basic American values, and if many Americans have so argued, then it is all the more surprising that some version of socialism, as the main alternative to capitalist economic organization in the modern world, has not found favor in the United States. Socialism has often seemed merely to compound the evil that is contained in capitalism. Rather than releasing the autonomous individual and placing him in a context of genuine participatory community, socialism has been seen as a system that crushes the individual under a centralized bureaucratic structure even more effectively than corporate capitalism. With the example of state socialism in the Soviet Union since 1917, that argument has been especially hard to refute. But there are concepts of socialism and socialist movements in the world that reject the Stalinist model. The American aversion to socialism goes deeper than rational argument. It is worth trying to understand the basis of that aversion, for such understanding will instruct us about some aspects of the American soul.

In 1887 Edward Bellamy's utopian novel *Looking Backward* described a society in which all the economic disturbances of his day had been overcome. In Bellamy's ideal society everyone served in the highly centralized economy for a maximum of 22 years and then enjoyed a life of leisure and self-expression on a fixed and equal income. Bellamy's book started a not inconsiderable movement of what came to be known as "Nationalist" clubs. In 1888 Bellamy explained why he avoided the term socialist:

In the radicalness of the opinions I have expressed I may seem to outsocialize the socialists, yet the word socialist is one I could never well stomach. It smells to the average American of petroleum, suggests the red flag and all manner of sexual novelties, and an abusive tone about God and religion. . . . Whatever German and French reformers may choose to call themselves, socialist is not a good name for a party to succeed with in America.[14]

In his very choice of the name "nationalist" Bellamy gave an indication of another feature of socialism that he was trying to disavow, namely that it is a foreign ideology, un-American.

It is true that socialism arrived in the United States in

the early 19th century as a revolutionary messianic ideology of French origin. As such it inevitably was seen as a rival and possibly a danger to America's own revolutionary messianic ideology. This rival ideology carried its own myth of origin quite different from ours. Early in the history of the new nation there had been a deep revulsion against the excesses of the French Revolution and a tendency to contrast it with the moderate and humane character of the American Revolution. Such a contrast was stated most vigorously by the early Federalists but was in some form or other accepted by Jeffersonian Democrats as well. How vivid was the memory of the French Revolution and how easily revolutionary socialism was identified with it is indicated by the fact that even Brownson's quite explicitly unsocialist proposals of 1840 earned for him the soubriquet of "Jacobin" or "the American Robespierre." The fact that later socialist ideologists in America were very frequently immigrants only added to the foreign image.

"Revolutionary" could never be an entirely negative attribute in America and if that were the only problem with socialism it is possible that it might have been domesticated. More serious is what Bellamy referred to as its "abusive tone about God and religion," namely the undeniable atheism and materialism that characterized not all kinds of socialism but particularly the most influential strand, Marxism. This was, and I suggest even now remains, a grave and serious stumbling block. In Europe not only many of the intellectuals but the mass of the workers tended to be disaffected with religion and alienated from the church in the 19th century, but not in America. Even though American intellectuals were ambivalent about the Protestant tradition, they showed an inveterate idealism to which the stress on material motivation of many socialists could only be abhorrent. Reacting against capitalist materialism such men were not apt to be attracted to socialist materialism. Indeed one may wonder whether, if Karl Marx had studied a little less at the feet of David Ricardo and a little more at the feet of William Blake, he might not have had a far more powerful impact on English-speaking intellectuals. But whatever was the case with the subtleties of the intellectuals, to the average American worker an ideology that claimed to be explicitly atheistic could only be repulsive.

Though "revolutionary" and "atheistic" would continue to be negative terms used to characterize socialism, it was the attribute of collectivism or statism, in contrast to allegedly American individualism, that would be the central negative image. This image, however, involved a double distortion. For one thing there were religious, democratic, and humanistic forms of socialism emphasizing individual dignity that Americans almost entirely failed to see or appreciate. For another the American tradition itself was not one-sidedly individualistic but always involved a balance of concern between the individual and his community. When the functions of political community were degraded to a matter of mere "police protection," both the tradition of the covenant community and of constitutional republicanism were subverted.

Inevitably when a dichotomy becomes magnified in such a way that both sides of it are distorted, one begins to suspect the presence of the psychological mechanism of projection. The "rugged individualist" decrying every form of collectivism, above all atheistic communism, as the very embodiment of evil, may be projecting his own dependency needs and needs for community, ruthlessly repressed and denied in himself, onto his alleged enemies. Even granted the unspeakable crimes committed in the 20th century by Communist nations (a close inspec-

tion of the history of the century, however, would dis-
close that such societies have had no monopoly on unspeakable crimes) the morbid anti-Communism of the
American right, and the tendency to assimilate every
kind of socialist or even liberal position to that of Communism, indicates, I believe, some serious failure to
come to terms with the balance between dependence and
independence, solidarity and autonomy, that are part of
any mature personality or society. This morbid obsession may be a symptom then, not of the genuine Americanism that it claims, but of its distortion and pathology.

5

A quick look at those brief moments in American history when socialism did strike a response tends to
confirm the above analysis of the reasons for its more
usual unpopularity. The varieties of socialism that attracted a flurry of interest in the second quarter of the
19th century, namely the theories of Robert Owen and
Charles Fourier, were not revolutionary in any violent
sense; they were easily reconciled with religious and
idealistic philosophies; and they each gave a high consideration to individual autonomy. A passage from Henry
James, Sr., father of Henry and William James, gives us
the flavor of a socialism that was, for a moment at least,
completely indigenized. James was a Swedenborgian
transcendentalist and a Fourierist socialist. On the question of property James wrote in the early 1850s:

Thus Socialism condemns, after a certain stage of human
progress, the institution of limited property. It demands for
man an infinite property, that is to say a property in universal
nature and in all the affections and thoughts of humanity. It
is silly to charge it with a tendency to destroy property. It aims
indeed to destroy all merely limited and conventional prop-

erty, all such property as is held not by any inward fitness of the subject, but merely by external police or convention; but it aims to destroy even this property only in the pacific way of superseding it, that is, by giving the subject possession of the whole earth, or a property commensurate with his inward and essential infinitude.[15]

In the first summer of the Civil War James was asked to give the Fourth of July address at Newport, Rhode Island. At that critical moment in history he chose to express his fundamental Americanism in socialist form:

I never felt proud of my country for what many seem to consider her prime distinction, namely, her ability to foster the rapid accumulation of private wealth. It does not seem to me a particularly creditable thing, that a greater number of people annually grow richer under our institutions than they do anywhere else. . . .

No; what makes one's pulse to bound when he remembers his own home under foreign skies, is never the rich man, nor the learned man, nor the distinguished man of any sort who illustrates its history, for in all these petty products almost every country may favorably, at all events tediously, compete with our own; but it is all simply the abstract manhood itself of the country, man himself unqualified by convention, the man to whom all these conventional men have been simply introductory, the man who—let me say it—for the first time in human history finding himself in his own right the peer of every other man, spontaneously aspires and attains to a far freer and profounder culture of his nature than has ever yet illustrated humanity. . . .

The letter kills, the spirit alone gives life; and it is exclusively to this undeniable spiritual difference between Europe and America, as organized and expressed in our own constitutional polity, that all our formal differences are owing. Our very Constitution binds us, that is to say, the very breath of our political nostrils binds us, to disown all distinctions among

men, to disregard persons, to disallow privilege the most established and sacred, to legislate only for the common good,
no longer for those accidents of birth or wealth or culture
which spiritually individualize man from his kind, but only for
those great common features of social want and dependence
which naturally unite him with his kind, and inexorably demand the organization of such unity. . . . The sentiment of
human unity, of the sole original sacredness of man and the
purely derivative sanctity of persons, no matter who they are,
is what we are born to, and what we must not fail to assert with
an emphasis and good-will which may, if need be, make the
world resound. For it is our very life, the absolute breath of our
nostrils, which alone qualifies us to exist.[16]

During the 1870s and 1880s the communitarian socialism of the period before the Civil War was almost
forgotten and most Americans writing on the subject
were pointing with alarm to the possibility of class warfare and destructive revolution that European socialism
would bring to America. Henry Ward Beecher saw socialism "drifting in from the eastern ocean like a New-
foundland fog."[17] But in fact virtually the only socialists
active in America in those years were a small group of
German immigrants who managed to strike remarkably
little response. As Albert Fried has suggested, one of the
reasons that the Marxian socialism preached by the Germans was so ineffective is that it seemed to most Americans "to lack a moral dimension."[18] Only gradually when
it became naturalized in native and moralistic form did
it, in the first decade and a half of the 20th century in the
guise of the Socialist Party of America, become a significant force on the American scene. Though its electoral
successes were widespread at the local and state level the
success of the early Socialist Party as a movement with
mass appeal was very much linked to the personality of
Eugene V. Debs who polled nearly a million votes in the

presidential campaign of 1912. Ralph Gabriel character-
izes Debs in a way that neatly suggests his appeal: "Debs,
the perennial candidate for president, was primarily an
evangelist of a humanitarian socialist gospel that emphasized the greed of the rich and the sufferings of the
poor."[19]

Debs was a Marxist of sorts but he was far more an
orator than a theoretician. He presented socialism in a
very American rhetoric, full of biblical imagery and
steeped in American history. He touched the old
springs of Protestant messianism, for example, when he
said:

The workers are the saviors of society; the redeemers of the
race; and when they have fulfilled their great historic mission,
men and women can walk the highlands and enjoy the vision
of a land without masters and without slaves, a land regener-
ated and resplendent in the triumph of freedom and civilization.[20]

He pitched his appeal on a high moral level, always
eschewing violence and hatred though himself not infre-
quently the subject of violence and hatred. "There is no
room in our hearts," he said, "for hatred, except for the
system. . . ."[21] And again:

Did the Socialist Party have no higher political ideal than the
victory of one class over another it would not be worthy of a
moment's support from any right-thinking individual. It
would, indeed, be impossible for the party to gain any considerable strength or prestige. It is the great moral worth of its
ideals that attracts adherents to the Socialist movement even
from the ranks of the capitalist class, and holds them to their
allegiance with an enthusiasm that suggests a close parallel
with the early days of Christianity. . . .[22]

Such words may appear naive to an orthodox Marxist but they had far more persuasive power in the American context than any orthodox Marxist has ever had.

6

The Socialist Party did not survive World War I as an effective political force. Its collapse is only the most dramatic of the many breaks in continuity that mark the history of socialism in America. This is certainly not the place to answer the vexing problem of what went wrong. We can only offer a few reflections. The World War and the Russian Revolution each dealt the movement a heavy blow. The party's opposition to the war alienated the Anglo-American intellectuals who had given it much of its visibility. Debs consistently opposed the war but had for some time ceased to be more than an eloquent spokesman for the movement.[23] He was alienated by the factional politics that plagued the party.

The Russian Revolution symbolically linked socialism with foreign revolutionaries in American eyes. By 1920 the Socialist Party and the incipient Communist Party were much more exclusively ethnic organizations than the pre-war Socialist Party had ever been. This development made especially visible the obstacles that America's cultural and ethnic divisions have placed in the way of effective opposition movements. The alliance between intellectuals and workers that seems so essential for a successful socialist movement was particularly hard to sustain where class differences were compounded by ethnic and racial differences. Critical Anglo-American intellectuals could not easily turn to nor be accepted by other racial and ethnic groups. Ethnic intellectuals were often seduced into general American culture, leaving behind the problems of their own more unfortunate compatriots. As a result the socialist education movements that were effective among European workers were much less successful here and labor organizations limited their goals to short-run economic benefits. In addition the dominant secularism of many of the immigrant socialist intellectuals did not sit well with the evangelical idealistic socialism of the old Americans.

The American Communist party never generated the broad popular support that the old Socialist party had. It always suffered from the suspicion of foreign control. In the 1930s and early 1940s it had selective appeal to many Americans, particularly to intellectuals who adopted their political stance for essentially idealistic reasons and managed to hide from themselves the realities of Stalinism. The collapse of the Communist party, due to inner disaffection and outer persecution after World War II, was another significant break in continuity. During the 1960s several varieties of socialist ideology emerged under the general rubric of the New Left. During the course of the decade the militancy of its rhetoric rose as its mass appeal correlatively declined but as is usual in the history of American socialism it was based far more on idealistic zeal than on class interest. The failure of both the Communist party and the New Left to link their socialism to any genuinely American pattern of values and attitudes, and the use of foreign categories to analyze American society, is typical of all but a few moments in the history of American socialism. That failure guarantees isolation and ineffectiveness even though the economic institutions of the country and its social and cultural life cry out for critical inspection from a radical perspective.

7

We must now consider the ways in which the system of corporate industry that has grown up in the last cen-

tury undermines essential American values and constitutional order. Both the Declaration of Independence and
the Constitution contain an implicit guarantee of the
natural right to property, and that right is explicitly
stated in the great 14th Amendment to the Constitution.
As we have seen, private productive property was held to
be the essential economic base of a free citizenry by most
social analysts of the early republic. The constitutional
guarantee of the right to property was long used as a
legal hedge to defend corporate industrial capitalism
from government regulation. But the fact remains that
the great expropriator of private property in America has
not been the state but corporate capitalism. From a nation of individual property holders—farmers, artisans,
and merchants—we have become a nation of bureaucratic wage earners, dependent on vast institutional
structures that we do not control. The last bastion of
American economic autonomy, the family farm, has long
been on the decline. In a great agricultural state like
California the individual farmer can barely survive in the
face of ever-expanding corporate agriculture, a corporate agriculture which, in the form of tax benefits, subsi-
dized water supplies, and other governmental aid, re-
ceives far more support from the state than the
autonomous farmer ever did. What is finally evident in
agriculture has long been true in the rest of the
economy. It is certain that such corporate management
of the economy has made us richer than when the
economy was largely in individual hands. But has it not,
as Jefferson and Brownson and Whitman feared, undermined the moral basis of our republican institutions?

Correlative with the decline of private property, at
least private property as the founding fathers knew it and
meant it, has come the great concentration of political
power in corporate hands, power that is not easily

brought to account by any form of democratic process. The copper strip mining that threatens to physically destroy the city of Butte, Montana, is paralleled by the even more destructive social strip mining that is overtaking a city like San Francisco. The sudden uncontrolled proliferation of high rise office buildings, many of them incredibly ugly and completely out of proportion to the rest of the city, brings in its wake devastating social and economic consequences. The city as an organic balance of economic and residential areas is disrupted. Families flee to the suburbs as residential taxes rise to pay for the services that must now be supplied to commuters. Poverty and crime fill the fringes of the expanding office district. The sterile tiers of vast office buildings replace the tangled cluttered life of Chinatown and other ethnic communities. Opposition is not lacking, but these buildings are sponsored by such giants as Bank of America and United States Steel. The immense wealth and power of these corporations entirely outweigh the interests of the people of San Francisco, and one of America's few beautiful cities slides ever closer to the ugliness, chaos, and despair of the ravaged cities of the East.

Decisions that in their general implications are profoundly political are made on the basis of economic considerations and decided by the balance of private economic power. Private profit outweighs public good. Nothing in the current American institutional order is capable of placing proper restraints on such tendencies. Labor unions often cooperate with business as in San Francisco where the building trades unions campaigned against the effort to establish a citywide height limitation. Regulatory agencies have a tendency to sink into lethargy as their funds prove inadequate to the job they are expected to do, or they turn out to be staffed by men drawn from the very industries they are ostensibly to regulate. These are not moral failings of the men involved; they are the inevitable outcome when private aggregations of power have obligations only to making a profit and not to the general welfare. And, whatever may have been the case earlier in American history, it is becoming clear that the tyranny of profit has set us on a most dangerous course. Our economy can only survive through constant expansion, whatever the ecological and social consequences of that expansion. Thus in any economic crisis it is not possible to say: we are rich enough, we are wasting resources enough, let us consider the conserving of resources, more adequate repair of present equipment, improved quality but reduced quantity in our style of life. No; the economy is like a heroin addict; only another shot of the very profit narcotic that creates a recession will get us out of it. But how many more belts of uncontrolled economic expansion will we be able to absorb before the social and ecological consequences totally undermine our democratic society, not to speak of our physical health?

Nor can we afford to overlook what our present form of economy is doing to public morals and republican virtue. We have spoken before of the balance between impulse and control, liberation and institutionalized liberty, as being essential to a free society. But we have, in advertising, one of the central institutions of our economy, an institution upon which we spend more than we do on all our educational institutions combined, and far more than we spend on our churches, and which systematically and incessantly works to undermine that balance. A century ago advertising as an institution scarcely existed. Today the average American has seen 350,000 television commercials before he graduates from high school. As David Potter has written:

. . . the traditional institutions have tried to improve man and to develop in him qualities of social value, though, of course, these values have not always been broadly conceived. The church has sought to inculcate virtue and consideration of others—the golden rule; the schools have made it their business to stimulate ability and to impart skills. . . .

In contrast with these, advertising has in its dynamics no motivation to seek the improvement of the individual or to impart qualities of social usefulness, unless conformity to material values may be so characterized. . . . What is basic is that advertising, as such, with all its vast power to influence values and conduct, cannot ever lose sight of the fact that it ultimately regards man as a consumer and defines its own mission as one of stimulating him to consume or to desire to consume.[24]

That happiness is to be attained through limitless material acquisition is denied by every religion and philosophy known to man but is preached incessantly by every American television set. What this does to the large portion of our population who have the resources to engage in the getting game is bad enough. What it does to millions who are marginal to our economy and can participate only vicariously in the great cornucopia is grim indeed, grim in inner disappointment and frustration, grim in the possibility of unrestrained violence. Few societies could imagine themselves surviving very long when one of their central institutions was advocating unrestrained greed. Are we so different from all other human societies?

But the blighting effect of advertising, itself the necessary child of the profit drive of corporate capitalism, goes beyond its own message to what it does to the culture, or what passes as such, for which it pays. Advertising money goes to whatever has the widest and most emotionally powerful appeal, to television rather than to magazines, and to those television programs that cater to unrestrained violence and insinuating sexuality rather than those that make any demand on the mature intellect or moral sensitivity. Thus the present American economic system, through one of its chief institutions, seems to be dedicated to the propagation of every one of the classic vices of mankind and to the relentless undermining of the values and virtues upon which this nation is built.

And what are the benefits that we are supposed to have gained from this insatiable economic system? Prosperity, abundance, wealth. Even leaving aside the question of the uneven distribution of this wealth we may still raise the question as to whether wealth is the unalloyed good or poverty the unalloyed evil that American society at present believes them to be. We tend to define poverty as a situation of material deficit. That, however, outside the significant but still quite small percentage of the population that is genuinely hungry, is not the real reason that poverty is unbearable. Poverty is a social and political status involving vulnerability to political and even police intervention in one's life and the lack of any effective power to assert one's wishes and needs. Poverty is bad mainly because it is a condition of powerlessness, not because, in America at least, it involves stark material want. When poverty is chosen, when it is a voluntary status, undertaken for some moral or religious end, it is often a state of joy rather than of suffering, as in the case of Thoreau at Walden, the Peace Corps worker, or the inhabitant of a rural commune. Where it does not have the meaning of political vulnerability and defenselessness, a life of material simplicity can be deeply rewarding and is indeed increasingly being chosen by America's young. There is every reason to believe that a life of material austerity, of pride and pleasure in the quality of workmanship rather than in the amount consumed, a life lived in a warm and supportive community, would be far healthier for our society, ecologically and sociologically, than our present dominant pattern of ever-accelerating consumption. But our economy could not survive a mass turn to voluntary poverty, however much our republican morality might be improved by such a turn, and our economy exerts all of its enormous power to prevent such a turn. I submit that of the several critical features of our present social situation that leads me to call it America's third time of trial this is the most decisive.

I do not know whether some sort of decentralized democratic socialism can supply a healthier economic base for the kind of change that seems necessary if we are to continue as a society of free men and women. I suspect that it can. I see no advantage in a precipitate shift from a bad system to one that we are not reasonably assured will not after all be worse. But it is time, it seems to me, for those who see the serious pass to which our society has come, and the major contribution our present economic system has made to our present troubles, to put aside the bailing wire and paper clips of liberal tinkering and consider whether much more drastic changes may not be needed. I am sure that the socialism being preached by the radical sectarians on the far left, modeled on the ideas of Fidel Castro or the thought of Mao Tse-tung, leaders of two societies about as different from the United States as it is possible to be, is not the answer. But I am also convinced that serious men, responsible men, concerned with the survival of our society in some form of recognizable continuity with its past, must with all due care and deliberation, turn now to the social and political drawing boards in order to draw up proposals of far-reaching scope to meet the far-reaching problems in which we are embroiled. I suspect that our difficulties

will soon become so critical that even respected states-
men will disregard the taboos of the past and begin talking about and helping to delineate a distinctively American socialism.

With Henry James, Sr. we can perhaps look forward to
the day when what he called "limited property" is su-
perseded and we come into our inheritance of the
"whole earth." Emerson stated the issue clearly when he
wrote:

As long as our civilization is essentially one of property, of
fences, of exclusiveness, it will be mocked by delusions. Our
riches will leave us sick; there will be bitterness in our laughter,
and our wine will burn our mouth. Only that good profits
which we can taste with all doors open, and which serves all
men.[25]

Not that that openness will be easy to attain. There are
enormous concentrations of economic, political, and
technological power that will react harshly to any challenge. Even when those who profit from the present
economic organization of American society have lost
confidence in their own vision, even when they see ever
more clearly the catastrophe that the single-minded pursuit of wealth and power is creating, they will not easily
relinquish their power. Not only clear rational alternatives to the present irrational economic order are
needed; political organization, whether in an old structure like the Democratic party or in some new structure,
will be needed. And that organization, that movement,
must be broad enough and deep enough to engage millions of Americans from a variety of cultural backgrounds at the deepest level of their personality. For that
the socialist vision must be linked once again, as it was
for Henry James, Sr. and Eugene Debs, with a vision that

is moral and religious as well as political. We now turn to a consideration of the resources for the renewal of the imagination in America that is the necessary precondition and accompaniment to any social transformation.

VI

The Birth of New
American Myths

1

In the messianic atmosphere surrounding the birth of
the republic it was common to refer to England, or
Europe generally, as Babylon, in contrast to the New
Jerusalem which was America. Today we hear angry
voices cry "Babylon" against America. William Blake,
who had a profound imaginative sense of the meaning of
America in the context of the revolutionary situation in
the Atlantic world, saw Albion as "aged ignorance" clipping the wings, or trying to, of youthful America. But
revolutionary youth too quickly turns into aged ignorance and today it is America that engages in clipping
wings. The covenant, as we have seen, was broken almost
as soon as it was made. For a long time Americans were
able to hide from that fact, to deny the brokenness. Today the broken covenant is visible to all.

In 1888 Whitman said, "America is really the great test
or trial case for all the problems and promises and specu-
lations of humanity and of the past and present." In the
1970s the eyes of all peoples are still upon us, trying to
discern how the great experiment in newness is faring.

History lays a heavy burden upon us and there is little ground for optimism. What Whitman wrote in *Democratic Vistas* a century ago is even more apt today:

> For history is long, long, long. Shift and turn the combinations of the statement as we may, the problem of the future of America, is in certain respects as dark as it is vast. Pride, competition, segregation, vicious wilfulness, and license beyond example, brood already upon us. Unwieldly and immense, who shall hold in behemoth? who bridle leviathan? Flaunt it as we choose, athwart and over the roads of our progress loom huge uncertainty, and dreadful, threatening gloom. It is useless to deny it: Democracy grows rankly up the thickest, noxious, deadliest plants and fruits of all—brings worse and worse invaders—needs newer, larger, stronger, keener compensations and compellers.
>
> Our lands, embracing so much, (embracing indeed the whole, rejecting none,) hold in their breast that flame also, capable of consuming themselves, consuming us all. Short as the span of our national life has been, already have death and downfall crowded close upon us—and will again crowd close, no doubt, even if warded off. Ages to come may never know, but I know, how narrowly during the late secession war . . . our Nationality, . . . just grazed, just by a hair escaped destruction. . . .
>
> Even today, amid these whirls, incredible flippancy, and blind fury of parties, infidelity, entire lack of first-class captains and leaders, added to the plentiful meanness and vulgarity of the ostensible masses—that problem, the labor question, beginning to open like a yawning gulf, rapidly widening every year—what prospect have we? We sail a dangerous sea of seething currents, cross and under-currents, vortices—all so dark, untried—and whither shall we turn? It seems as if the Almighty had spread before this nation charts of imperial destinies, dazzling as the sun, yet with many a deep intestine difficulty, and human aggregate of cankerous imperfection,—saying, lo! the roads, the only plans of development, long and

varied with all terrible balks and ebullitions. You said in your soul, I will be empire of empires, overshadowing all else, past and present, putting the history of old-world dynasties, conquests behind me, as of no account—making old history a dwarf—I alone inaugurating largeness, culminating time. If these, O lands of America, are indeed the prizes, the determinations of your soul, be it so. But behold the cost, and already specimens of the cost. Thought you greatness was to ripen for you like a pear? If you would have greatness, know that you must conquer it through ages, centuries—must pay for it with a proportionate price. For you too, as for all lands, the struggle, the traitor, the wily person in office, scrofulous wealth, the surfeit of prosperity, the demonism of greed, the hell of passion, the decay of faith, the long postponement, the fossil-like lethargy, the ceaseless need of revolutions, prophets, thunderstorms, deaths, births, new projections and invigorations of ideas and men.[1]

Certainly today we stand in need of those new invigorations and new projections. The burden of the present with all its special problems makes us wonder about our past. What does it mean to us? How can we appropriate it? In 1926, while working on his great mythic poem, "The Bridge," Hart Crane expressed one side of the problem: "The form of my poem rises out of a past that so overwhelms the present with its worth and vision that I'm at a loss to explain my delusion that there exist any real links between that past and a future destiny worthy of it."[2] And yet, out of what we know now, comes the opposite doubt: Amid the pride, sin, weakness, and error of our past is there any strength for us? Is there a foundation on which to build?

The recognition of the broken covenant does not mean to me the rejection of the American past. We are not innocent, we are not the saviors of mankind, and it is well for us to grow up enough to know that. But there have been Americans at every point in our history who have tried to pick up the broken pieces, tried to start again, tried once more to build an ethical society in the light of a transcendent ethical vision. That too is part of our tradition, and if we can find no sustenance there, our prospect is even darker than it now seems.

2

Today the American civil religion is an empty and broken shell. It was from the beginning an external covenant. That in itself is no fault, for external covenants are necessary. Until we are all as angels, external law and restraint are essential for any kind of social existence. But in a republic an external covenant alone is never enough. It is of the nature of a republic that its citizens must love it, not merely obey it. The external covenant must become an internal covenant and many times in our history that has happened. In a series of religious and ethical revivals, that external covenant has become filled with meaning and devotion. Even though that inner meaning and devotion has often been betrayed, genuine achievements have been left behind. It is better that slavery has been abolished. It is better that women have the vote. But the internal covenant can never be completely captured by institutions; its life is that of the spirit and it has its own rhythms.

What we face today, however, is not simply a low ebb in that spiritual rhythm such as we have faced many times before. It is not that our external covenant is performing its function while waiting once again to be filled with a new measure of devotion. The external covenant has been betrayed by its most responsible servants and, what is worse, some of them, including the highest of all, do not even seem to understand what they have betrayed. Nor can we discount the events that were disclosed in the second presidential term of Richard Nixon as the work of a small band of wicked men. The men in question, it seems, were not notably more wicked than other Americans. When the leaders of a republic no longer understand its principle it is because of a history of corruption and betrayal that has affected the entire society.

The New England Puritans were certain that a broken covenant would not go unpunished. Lincoln in his Second Inaugural Address spoke of the retribution that was being exacted from the nation because of slavery. It is not easy to discern the workings of Providence. But is it not possible that our punishment for breaking the covenant is to be the most developed, progressive, and modern society in the world? What those adjectives point to is utter devastation—of the natural world in which we live, of the ties that bind us to others, of the innerness of spiritually sensitive personality, as we have seen in earlier chapters. Our punishment, ironically, lies in our "success," and that too not for the first time in history.[3]

If our economic and technological advance has placed power in the hands of those who are not answerable to any democratic process; weakened our families and neighborhoods as it turned individuals into mobile, competitive achievers; undermined our morality and stripped us of tradition—as I think it has—then we must consider where else to turn. It is natural that we should turn to tradition in time of need. But our relation to tradition, which is the subject of this book, is an ambiguous one. On the one hand our ties to tradition, whatever religious or ethnic group we come from, have been enormously eroded in the last century by the advance of modernization. For that reason any living link to tradition is precious. But on the other hand, in many curious ways, tradition is the cause of our present condition. Our reappropriation of tradition then must be in a sense "negative"—that is, critical—recognizing the broken-ness with the wholeness, the defeat with the victory. Above all any reappropriation of tradition must be made in the full consciousness of our present experience of loss. In these ways an authentic reappropriation is the direct opposite of the nostalgic, sentimental, and uncritical presentation of tradition in the mass media. They offer tradition as palliative. We need tradition as stimulus to rebirth.

3

The delineation of tradition in every chapter of this book has been critical. But perhaps we need to dwell for a few pages more on that moment of negativity that is so essential in our coming to terms with our history. "Success" with all its ambiguities has been the main story. Perhaps we need to look a little more explicitly at defeat. If we are to free ourselves for the future we must remember what we would rather forget.

Defeat is not a common experience in America, or perhaps I should say it is not a majority experience, and there have been many ways to mitigate its consequences. When the going got tough Roger Williams could go to Rhode Island and Jonathan Edwards could go to Stockbridge. The history of the Mormons is one of the most instructive in this regard.[4] The Church of Jesus Christ of Latter Day Saints was the largest and most successful of all the 19th-century communitarian experiments, and its history is almost a paradigm of that of the nation. Harassed in New York and Ohio, the early Mormons under Joseph Smith moved to Missouri. Driven out of Missouri, they built their thriving city of Nauvoo in Illinois. With the prophet murdered and Nauvoo burned, they set out in the dead of winter under the leadership of Brigham Young to cross the prairies and the mountains and found a new Zion in Utah. There they established an independent and self-maintaining agricultural society only very loosely under American governmental control. In the 1880s they were finally defeated in Utah too and lost their economic independence to the superior power of the dominant society. But once again they adapted, making a virtue of their economic marginality to carve a secure place in the larger society. Today they have almost obliterated from their memory the experience of one of the most crushing series of persecutions and defeats any community has ever suffered at the hands of the American government.

Others have not been so fortunate and have had to give defeat a more unflinching look. The South in the Civil War was the only part of our nation ever to experience directly the devastation of modern warfare in what was one of the largest and most destructive of 19th-century wars. While an indelible consciousness of defeat has lingered in the South it was softened by two contrasting strategies: one was the sentimentalization and glorification of the "lost cause"; the other was the identification with the aggressor which has made Southerners among the most nationalistic and militaristic supporters of American imperialism. However, in the work of William Faulkner, perhaps the only 20th-century novelist worthy of standing beside Hawthorne and Melville, the southern sense of defeat has been deepened into a genuine apprehension of tragedy, not so much by dwelling on the actual military defeat as by an unsparing delineation of the triumph of rapacious commercial values that followed it. Faulkner's description of the rape of the land, the destruction of a stubborn and hard-pressed peasantry, and the corruption of the southern middle and upper classes by those values transcends its particularly southern context and applies to America generally.[5]

Without any question it is the racial minorities—Indians, blacks, Mexican Americans, and Asian Americans—who have known defeat most deeply, most bitterly, and most continuously in American history. It is only in the last ten years that we have begun to become aware, partially and ambiguously, of the spiritual meaning of those defeats. There is of course more than one way to respond to radical defeat. One response is sheer disintegration and its spiritual expression a wordless scream. American history is punctuated with such screams out of the darkness. Another way, as with the South after the Civil War, is to identify with the aggressor and parody the worst aspects of the dominant system. Oppression often dehumanizes and there is nothing to be gained from hiding that fact. But there is the possibility of a third response. In the face of defeat one can attempt to build and maintain some kind of community that will not only aid in physical survival but be a model of human values in stark contrast to the oppressing society. Such efforts are likely to fail more often than they succeed, but even the defeats can be instructive. Many examples could be discussed, but I would like to consider one from that group whose present existence is perhaps the most damning testimony against the course of American history: the American Indian.

It would be instructive to analyze the Second Battle of Wounded Knee. Its effort to create community in the face of suspicion, its combination of idealism and despair, its testimony to the corruption of both oppressor and oppressed, and its tragic heroism in trying to actualize human values against impossible odds is a kind of microcosm of much of American history, but it would take a book to do it justice. Instead I would like to take the simpler but no less stark example of the death of Larry Casuse.[6]

On the first morning of March 1973, Larry Casuse, a young Navaho student at the University of New Mexico, entered the office of Frankie Garcia, mayor of Gallup, and put a gun to the mayor's head. He marched the mayor to a nearby sporting goods store which was quickly surrounded by police. The mayor escaped by jumping through a window and Larry Casuse was shot to death. Exactly what this previously peaceful young Navaho had in mind was not clear. Perhaps he wanted to hold the mayor hostage to negotiate about Indian problems in Gallup. Perhaps he merely wanted to humiliate the mayor and show the often humiliated Indian population that officials are only human. Certainly, if his intention had been murder, he could have carried it out easily. Some observers saw his action as suicidal from the beginning.

Larry Casuse was born and grew up in Gallup and his effort to learn about the traditional Navaho way had only begun in adolescence. He had become fascinated with the Navaho ideal of harmony with nature and man and the contrast to that ideal that American society presented. He became president of the Kiva Club, the Indian society at the University of New Mexico, and guided its interest toward both a recovery of traditional Indian thought and efforts to improve the conditions of Indians in American society. Larry and his friends were intrigued with the Navaho conception of "false people," so lacking in human feeling and so hypocritical that they can scarcely be considered human. Frankie Garcia, the mayor of Gallup, was a prime example of such a false person because, while owner of a tavern catering to Indians, he was chairman of an alcoholism project. When Garcia was nominated as a regent of the University of New Mexico, Larry Casuse went to Santa Fe to testify against the nomination. "The man is an owner of the

Navaho Inn, where numerous alcoholics are born, yet he ironically is chairman of the alcohol-abuse rehabilitation committee," he told the senators. "Does he not abuse alcohol? Does he not abuse it by selling it to intoxicated persons who often end up in jail or a morgue from over-exposure?"[7]

When Garcia's nomination as a regent was confirmed by the legislature in January, Larry Casuse was very bitter. That may have helped bring on the March 1 confrontation. After his death a statement from the Kiva Club, addressed to "All Human Beings," said, "The real issue is not who-shot-whom, as the national media seem to imply, but rather why Larry Casuse so willingly sacrificed his life in order to communicate with the world his dream of unifying human beings with Mother Earth, the Universe, and Humanity."[8] We may agree that Larry Casuse died for a conception of community that he found sadly lacking in his social environment. But we must also ask why his action so utterly violated his own ideals. He made the classic American mistake of defining his community too exclusively, distinguishing too radically the subhuman "false people" from the "Human Beings."

We have said that defeat in America has not been a majority experience. American history has usually been presented as a great "success story," and much in that story is true. But there has been a compulsive concentration on the means of attaining success with little concern about the broader terms in which success is to be measured. William James warned us about the pitfalls of this compulsive preoccupation, what he called the worship of the bitch-goddess SUCCESS, around the turn of the century. But Americans have not wanted to hear about pitfalls. They have been compulsively afraid of defeat and have preferred to banish "negative thinking" from their consciousness while they magically reiterate the theme of self-confidence and victory. But in the late decades of the 20th century it is becoming increasingly difficult to exercise that form of mind control. The shadow of defeat keeps appearing, as I have suggested, not somewhere at the periphery but in the very midst of our alleged success. A nation that has never known anything but military victory has recently twice had to settle for a draw, not because we have really been beaten, but because our very intoxication with our own power has led us into untenable situations where the cost of "victory" became so great that it was no longer tolerable. The illusion that our power allows us to be the world's policeman is now gone and there is the growing realization that our relative power in the world is in decline.

But far more serious are the inner problems that we face at home. Mostly brought on by our long love affair with economic development without adequate attention to anything else, there are everywhere signs of ecological and social breakdown. The economy itself seems unresponsive to the "fine tuning" of the new economics or to the cruder measures of the old. As our defeats and failures become ever harder to deny, the specter of complete collapse looms on the horizon. We may indeed, as John Winthrop warned, "perish out of this good land whither we passed over the vast sea to possess it." Or perhaps we may still gain some wisdom by looking at the abyss, which has been there all the time but which we in America have for so long steadfastly refused to see.

Of course, not all Americans, even in the majority community, have refused to see. The Puritan fathers were quite aware of the darkness that is so important a part of human existence, and even in the 19th century, when progressive optimism seemed to carry all before it, there were those who saw the truth. The personal experience of our greatest artists revealed to them that to which their compatriots remained blind. Hawthorne, for example, in 1859, on the very verge of the Civil War, saw "that pit of blackness that lies beneath us, everywhere. The firmest substance of human happiness," he said, "is but a thin crust spread over it, with just reality enough to bear up the illusive stage scenery amid which we tread. It needs no earthquake to open the chasm. A footstep, a little heavier than ordinary, will serve; and we must step very daintily, not to break through the crust at any moment. By and by, we inevitably sink!"[9] In 1876 Melville, in describing the happy domestic scene of a mother and child, remarked, "Under such scenes abysses be—/ Dark quarries where few care to pry."[10] Perhaps he remembered that day not ten years before when his own eldest son, 18 years old, shot himself to death in his room at home. But deep as was the sense of personal tragedy in Hawthorne and Melville, it was part of a larger vision of social tragedy. Both men worried deeply about the future of their society. Melville expressed his concern about the coming "Dark Ages of Democracy," since the New World had come too suddenly "to share old age's pains—/ To feel the arrest of hope's advance." And then mankind will hear the sad cry, "No New World to mankind remains!"[11] Melville already foreshadows the transformation of New Jerusalem into Babylon.

Melville and Hawthorne were able to turn their own defeats, their own experiences of nothingness, into great art. Their art was not only a personal triumph but a social triumph, for it showed that even in this raw new country tragic understanding was possible. How can we today turn the defeat that hangs over us, the defeat that ripens in the very midst of our "success," into understanding and action? For that we need also the life-giving, positive aspect of tradition that was much closer and more accessible to Hawthorne and Melville than it is to us. We need to see as they did that the negative and the affirmative aspects of tradition are not ultimately separate. Only through a sense of tragedy is it possible to be instructed by the past. But for them tradition was still something lived, complex as their relation to it was. For us tradition is on the way to becoming something we know about but do not live. While our knowledge is more complete and more accurate than ever before, it is also disembodied, alienated from our daily lives. Our lives are largely ruled by an insistent commercial culture that is a parody of any tradition. We need to consider then, not only what can speak to us, but how to make it genuinely our own.

4

As a first step, I would argue, we must reaffirm the outward or external covenant and that includes the civil religion in its most classical form. The Declaration of Independence, the Bill of Rights, and the Fourteenth Amendment to the Constitution have never been fully implemented. Certainly the words "with liberty and justice for all" in the Pledge of Allegiance are not factually descriptive. But while I can understand the feeling of a Garrison that such hypocritically employed documents should be rejected, I would follow the course of a Weld and insist that they be fulfilled. If they have never been completely implemented, neither have they been entirely without effect. If the liberty they protect is largely negative, largely a defense against encroachment, it is still the indispensable condition for the attainment of any fuller freedom. It is for this reason that the reassertion of constitutional principles in the face of the recent challenge is so essential. If we allow the external covenant to be subverted utterly, then our task is infinitely greater: not to renew a republic, but to throw off a despotism. Given the technical resources of the modern

world, challenging a despotism is overwhelmingly difficult. But to stop at the reaffirmation of the external covenant may ultimately defeat even that goal.

The defense of negative freedom, of civil rights and
liberties, while ignoring massive injustice, poverty, and
despair will be self-defeating. Negative freedom only defends the individual against incursions, whereas positive
freedom actually creates the conditions for the full participation of all. Positive freedom, what Jefferson called
public freedom, has always been an element in American
political life, even though its meaning has changed over
time. That larger freedom that not only defends self-
interest, as negative freedom does, but fulfills it in the
common good, is the essence of the inward or internal
covenant. It is to that end that revivals, reawakenings,
and renewals have occurred. As part of the increasing
dominance of technical reason the idea has grown up, at
least in the 20th century, that positive freedom is a
purely technical problem, one that should be left to the
experts and the bureaucrats to solve. Matters of "public
policy" have been seen as largely instrumental, involving
the effective use of means. However, cut off from some
larger end that is understood and internalized by the
society as a whole, and particularly by the recipients of
the public policy in question, purely technical and ad-
ministrative solutions have again and again broken
down. Instead of solving problems they have only
created new ones, as in the cases of urban renewal and
the welfare system. Once again we find that the autonomous technical reason that is the basis of our "success"
carries the seeds of our doom.

It is not technical reason as such that is at fault but the
fact that it has come unhinged from a larger religious and
moral context. Technical reason can never tell us about
ends, and the public freedom we need is always related

to that *telos,* that end, in terms of which society as a whole makes sense. But how do we know that end? Neither sociology nor economics nor political science nor even law and government can teach it to us, though we may hope that they are all informed by it. There are two ways we can know the end. One is through tradition, or that part of tradition, myth, that summarizes the deepest experiences of the group. Myth tells the story of those encounters that are considered sacred because they have revealed what reality is and how we should act in relation to it. The other way is through reason, not technical reason but that more comprehensive reason that gives us knowledge of the whole, what can be called transcendental reason or ecstatic reason. As examples of ecstatic reason we might cite Plato's vision of the Good, Spinoza's intellectual love of God, or Edwards's and Backus's love of Being and all beings.[12]

In a period like our own, when we have lost our sense of direction, when we do not know where our goal is, when our myths have lost their meaning and comprehensive reason has been eclipsed by calculating technical reason, there is need for a rebirth of imaginative vision. In the face of such a situation imagination can sometimes fuse myth and ecstatic reason to render a new vision, a new sense of direction and goal. Such a new vision is never unrelated to older visions—that is why tradition is so important; but neither is it identical with them—that is why ecstatic reason must also be involved.

Given the dominance of technical reason, it might be assumed that our society would be suffering from a great dearth of imaginative vision. It is true that spiritual aridity is widespread in many sectors of our society, but if we look more closely we will see that rather than a dearth there is a superabundance of competing visions. The late 6os saw a spiritual ferment that has been compared to a great awakening. Even though the cultural revolution of that period seems to have prematurely withered, new religious groups, often with a small but fervent following, continue to proliferate.

5

The religious movements that grow while the established religious bodies continue to decline share one thing in common: they take a dim view of contemporary American society. In spite of great diversity of origin and symbol, and widely varying degrees of spiritual sensitivity, most of them are not only critical but contain an apocalyptic or millennial note. The numerous followers of Yogi Bhajan see the present as the last degenerate stage of a 2,000-year-old Piscean Age, into which the new Aquarian Age is about to dawn. The Hare Krishna chanters see the world at the end of the materialistic Kali-Yuga, the last cycle in a four-cycle sequence, and predict the coming of a new age of peace and happiness. The world gathering of the followers of Majaraj Ji in Houston was called Millennium '73. And many Pentecostal and Jesus groups see the present in biblical terms as the end of times just before Jesus is to return.

The apocalyptic note extends well beyond religious groups proper and affects many secular critics of contemporary America as well. Secular critics share with religious critics much the same image of what is wrong with present America whether they see the new age in terms of "body awareness" and "sensitivity training" or socialist revolution. Exotic as their background may be, all these critics of the present are part of a tradition that goes back continuously to the beginning of the settlement of America. Another element of continuity, conscious or not, is the idea that they are a remnant, a people called out of the larger doomed society to herald a new age.

Much of the content of the criticism of American society is familiar. It sees America as infatuated with materialism, on a "power trip" or an "ego trip," trying to force its will on nature, other societies, and the deep interior of the self. The dominance of technical reason, the success ideal, and control by unresponsive bureaucracies, aspects of American society discussed in this book, are frequently mentioned by these critics. But some go much further and turn away not only from modern America but from the whole Western tradition. They reject biblical religion and choose instead one of South or East Asian origin. In so doing they reject a biblical conception of God and the idea of obedience to God as the chief form of religious action. Rather they emphasize the experience of mystical illumination and seek in their religious action to overcome all dualisms and find unity with nature and the universe. They deny the clear distinction between God and the self that is so central in biblical religion. Many of them also reject the mastery of humans over nature and of men over women and children that biblical religion has often nurtured. On the latter point the evidence is ambiguous, since masculine dominance has frequently been part of oriental religion. But westerners have drawn what they saw as the clear implications of these traditions for sex relationships less informed by masculine dominance. When western female Zen masters were ordained in Japan, something without traditional warrant, there was no objection. If the biblical tradition has been rejected so has the Greek. The obligation to give a clear intellectual account of one's faith, one of the Greek elements in western religion, is not felt as compelling by those who have taken up oriental cults. The emphasis is rather on direct experience, unmediated by reflective intelligence. The oriental traditions too have their intellectual tradition but in America today there is much less emphasis on studying the sutras, say, than on the practice of meditation.

Interest in oriental religion goes back in America to the early 19th century, as we have seen, but never before have significant numbers of people gone beyond reading books to become adepts and engage in arduous practice. The followers of oriental religions are still few, perhaps less than one per cent nationally, but they are from a strategic group. They come by and large from the most privileged, best educated strata of American youth. They include many who would have been expected to excel in conventional career patterns. A negative attitude toward established American economic and political institutions is clearer among those practicing oriental disciplines than among those who are drawn into new forms of Christian community. Many of the former have chosen to live communally and to work in nonprofessional occupations in order to make the collective self-sufficient. Many turn to manual jobs or crafts and some in rural communes engage in farming. They reject mass culture along with the dominant economic system and create their own art, music, and festivities. In all these ways they demonstrate a clear witness in opposition to the major trends of American society.

The followers of oriental religions are in a sense counterparts to and sometimes refugees from radical political groups that have been active in America since the early 60s. They share much the same analysis of American society and culture though they have adopted a different strategy. Those among the older established religious groups who have become dissatisfied with conventional religiosity may also be divided into those opting for direct political action and those seeking to form new religious communities. Jews, Catholics, and Protestants have been led by the ethical demands of their faith to direct political action, as in the case of the Berrigans and William Sloan Coffin. Others have found in the recent disarray of American society occasion to intensify their specifically religious commitment. Hasidism has had an appeal to young Jews as have Pentecostal and Jesus movements to Catholics and Protestants. While often not sharing the radical political views of their activist coreligionists, they too tend to withdraw from the main society, establish separate social and cultural enclaves, and await a better time.

While this spiritual ferment does not threaten the established order, it does signal a shift in the main line of American culture. Now, as before in American history, the still small voice that is heard only by the spiritually sensitive may portend seismic changes for the society as a whole. The dominant liberal utilitarian culture has been challenged many times but perhaps never by such an array of political and religious alternatives. While it would not be true to say that faith in technical reason is dead, it has sustained a succession of severe shocks. Many Americans, more than in a long time, have come to feel that our problems do not arise merely from a faulty choice of means but from a failure of our central vision. They seek a new or renewed vision and turn to the great myths and symbols of the world's religions to find it. In humanistic psychology and in certain areas of philosophy, anthropology, literary criticism, and religious studies concerned with the meaning and function of myth and symbol, there is a return to comprehensive or holistic reason, a new emphasis on the immediacy of experience, that makes the appropriation of religious traditions more possible for educated people than has been the case for a long time.[13]

Much that is happening can be understood in terms of the Protestant conversion/covenant pattern—even when it does not use that language. But there is a renewal of the sources of religious imagination that have been dry for two centuries. Most of that renewal has come from outside the Protestant tradition—from the oriental emphasis on immediate experience and harmony with nature, from the Catholic emphasis on community and the sacramental life, from the Jewish experience of keeping the faith in the midst of disaster. But the millennial note, the ethical criticism of society, and the insistence on the role of a remnant that already embodies the future, are thoroughly in consonance with the central theme of the American Protestant experience.[14]

6

In spite of these voices in the wilderness, the main drift of American society is to the edge of the abyss. Nor are the new developments entirely without problems.

I think we must distinguish between core and periphery in the social criticism of America. At the core are those actually experimenting in a serious and disciplined way with new forms of community and symbolic expression. A much larger number, however, perhaps a majority of a whole generation, has been influenced by the criticism of the old order but has accepted no new discipline in its stead. For them the critical rhetoric may simply reinforce the narrow individualism and concern with self-interest that is the underside of the old American tradition, but now with few ethical restraints, because the older social justifications have lost their legitimacy. Some critics of American society welcome this erosion of all normative order in the society and see it as a prelude to "revolution." I do not. Cynicism and moral anarchism, whether expressed in crimes against persons and property by the dispossessed or in self-interested manipulation by the better-off, are, if I read modern history right, more likely a prelude to authoritarianism if not fascism. Those who would criticize all the accepted conventions of our society—all the inherited obligations to family, friends, work and country —as "bourgeois" may be sowing bitter seeds. A period of great social change always produces a certain amount of antinomianism and anarchism. But by that very token a time of great change is a time of great danger. Change can be, as anyone who reads the 20th century can see, for the worse as well as for the better.

What I am calling the "core groups," those actually trying to live a new vision, give hope in that they are actually working out a new balance of impulse and control, energy and discipline, rather than abandoning all control and discipline. But here too there are problems. In the great welter of urban and rural communes, political and religious collectives, sects, cults, and churches that have sprung up in recent years, there are many interesting developments. A new balance of manual and mental labor, work and celebration, male and female traits have been experimented with. Harmony with nature and one's own body, a more "feminine" and less dominating attitude toward one's self and others, an ability to accept feelings and emotions—including feelings of weakness and despair—a willingness to accept personal variety, have all been valued and tried in practice. Elsewhere I have indicated that whereas biblical religions are oriented to a sky god, the new religions, explicitly or implicitly, seem more oriented to an earth goddess:

Unlike the religions of the sky father this tradition celebrates Nature as a mother. The sky religions emphasize the paternal, hierarchical, legalistic and ascetic, whereas the earth tradition emphasizes the maternal, communal, expressive and joyful aspects of existence. Whereas the sky religions see fathers, teachers, rulers and gods exercising external control through laws, manipulation or force, the earth tradition is tuned to cosmic harmonies, vibrations and astrological influences. Socially the [earth tradition] expresses itself not through impersonal bureaucracy or the isolated nuclear family but through collectives, communes, tribes and large extended families.[15]

The very extent to which these new emphases are merely the reversed image of the old ones raises questions. Much of the "counterculture" was the bringing to consciousness of what was present but repressed in old American culture, and most followers of the counterculture have all the old traits present but repressed in themselves. The willingness to actually experiment with new forms of personal and social existence has been most valuable. Ideas that are not lived are seldom effective. But one may doubt that a synthesis adequate to our problems has yet been attained. Probably more of the old biblical culture needs to be included in a new pattern for America than the counterculture would allow. The Jesus movements have not made the synthesis either, for they have not really absorbed the new challenge to the inherited culture.

Lived experimentation with new forms is one of the few hopeful things in contemporary America. We may learn much from it. But the results are not all in, and the transferability of small group patterns to the whole society may turn out to be slight. For example, recent experiments with new patterns of authority seem to show, just as did similar communitarian experiments in the 19th century, that the more egalitarian the group, the more ephemeral it is. Groups with strong leaders, unquestioned authority, rituals and ethical codes seen as beyond doubt seem more likely to survive over time. Such authoritarian patterns can be quite oppressive within the group, but since members can leave to return to the larger society or to find a more congenial group, there are limits to their despotic potential. But America under the leadership of the Maharaj Ji or America organized along the lines of the Children of God, would not be a pleasing prospect.

While decentralization and community decision-making are in themselves a valuable lesson for the larger society, the kind of socialism that marks the practical existence of small groups cannot be simply generalized to the nation. Communes provide few clues to the re-organization of large-scale industry, technology, and science that are needed if we are to survive our third time of trial.

The emphasis on experience and practice in the new groups is among their most valuable contributions, but they are not greatly helpful with the larger intellectual problems that face us. A serious intellectual critique of our society must be based on a fuller analysis than most of them have made. They may contribute to that revival of comprehensive reason that could lead us to a new sense of social *telos*, but alone they are not likely to create it. Their abstention from mass culture is admirable, though the temptations toward co-optation are great. But they have not done more than create a stimulus toward a larger cultural revival. Finally, their concerns are personal, local, and universal but seldom national; and many of our severest problems can only be handled at the national level.

Valuable as the current group experimentation is, it alone will not solve our problems. Only a national move-ment, by which I do not mean a single national organiza-

tion, can begin to meet these problems. Such a movement would have a political, I believe socialist, side. It
would also have an intellectual and a religious side.
Whatever we might wish, the national community exer-
cises control over our fate and in part over the fate of the
world. It is our moral responsibility as Americans not to
give up the struggle at the national level. As I have argued throughout this book, critical Americans must not
leave the tradition of American idealism entirely to the
chauvinists. The history of modern nations shows that
segmentary rational politics is not enough. No one has
changed a great nation without appealing to its soul,
without stimulating a national idealism, as even those
who call themselves materialists have discovered. Culture is the key to revolution; religion is the key to culture.
If we win the political struggle, we will not even know
what we want unless we have a new vision of man, a new
sense of human possibility, and a new conception of the
ordering of liberty, the constitution of freedom. Without
that, political victory, even were it attainable, could have
no lasting result.

7

The present spiritual condition of America is not very
cheering. Melville wrote of our condition more than a
century ago when he spoke of landlessness: "as in landlessness alone rests highest truth, shoreless, indefinite as
God—so better is it to perish in that howling infinite,
than be ingloriously dashed upon the lee, even if that
were safety."[16] Landlessness is a condition of being "at
sea" and that is where we are, and in a rising storm. If
the storm wakes us from false innocence, makes us see
our world as it is and not as we blindly wished it to be,
then it may be the beginning of liberation. We certainly
need a new "Great Awakening." The inward reform of

conversion, the renewal of an inward covenant among the remnant that remains faithful to the hope for rebirth, is more necessary than it has ever been in America. The great experiment may fail utterly, and such failure will have dark consequences not only for Americans but for all the world.

We should not be so overawed by the late American worship of technical reason that we enter once again the illusion of omnipotence. One of the tenets of the early Puritans that we could well remember is that the millenium is brought by God, not man. Above all, Americans need to learn how to wait as well as to act. We have plunged into the thickets of this world so vigorously that we have lost the vision of the good. We need to take time again to see visions and dream dreams. But as Plato wrote so long ago, the vision of the good does not exempt us from life in the cave. Faith is not utilitarian but neither is it an escape from the search for the useful.

We do not know what the future holds and we must give up the illusion that we control it, for we know that it depends not only on our action but on grace. While recognizing the reality of death, we may return finally to Winthrop's biblical injunction:

Let us choose life.

Notes

PREFACE

1. Jurgen Habermas describes the method of the "historic-hermeneutic sciences" as follows: "The world of traditional meaning discloses itself to the interpretor only to the extent that his own world becomes clarified at the same time. The subject of understanding establishes communication between both worlds. He comprehends the substantive content of tradition by *applying* tradition to himself and his situation." *Knowledge and Human Interests*, Beacon, 1971, pp. 309–310.

2. There is no need to repeat here autobiographical details that have already been included in the Introduction to my *Beyond Belief: Essays on Religion in a Post-Traditional World*, Harper and Row, 1970.

I   AMERICA'S MYTH OF ORIGIN

1. See also the following articles of mine on this subject: "Civil Religion in America," *Daedalus*, Winter, 1967; "Evil and the American Ethos," in *Sanctions for Evil*, Nevitt Sanford and Craig Comstock (eds.), Jossey-Bass, 1971; "American Civil Religion in the 1970s," *Anglican Theological Review*, Supplementary Series, No. 1, July, 1973; "Reflections on Reality in America," *Radical Religion*, Vol. 1, No. 3, 1974; "Religion and Polity in America," *Andover Newton Quarterly*, Vol. 15, No. 2, 1974. Portions of "Religion and Polity" appear in Chapter 1 and a portion of "Reflections" appears in Chapter 6 of this book.

2. Hannah Arendt, *On Revolution*, Viking Compass, 1965, p. 214.

3. On this point Hannah Arendt has the following to say: "The great measure of success the American founders could book for

themselves, the simple fact that the revolution here succeeded where all others were to fail, namely in founding a new body politic stable enough to survive the onslaught of centuries to come, one is tempted to think, was decided the very moment when the Constitution began to be 'worshiped,' even though it had hardly begun to operate." *Ibid.,* p. 199.

4. John Locke, *The Second Treatise of Government,* 49, 1.

5. Quoted in James Sellers, *Public Ethics,* Harper and Row, 1970, p. 169. It is interesting to note, in passing, that Santayana described in 1920 as a permanent feature of the American character what some observers today mistakenly believe is only characteristic of the current younger generation.

6. John Locke, *Second Treatise,* 2, 4–9.

7. Howard Mumford Jones, *O Strange New World,* Viking Compass, 1967, pp. 15–16.

8. George H. Williams, *Wilderness and Paradise in Christian Thought,* Harper Bros., 1962, p. 101.

9. Mircea Eliade, *The Quest: History and Meaning in Religion,* University of Chicago Press, 1969, p. 94.

10. In this section I am very much dependent on Gerhart B. Ladner, *The Idea of Reform,* Harper Torchbook, 1967 (Harvard University Press 1959).

11. On typological interpretation in early Christianity and the Middle Ages see the classic article of Erich Auerbach, "Figura," first published in German in 1944 and available in English in Erich Auerbach, *Scenes from the Drama of European Literature,* Meridian Books, 1959, pp. 11–76. For the Puritan use of this mode of interpretation see Robert Middlekauff, *The Mathers,* Oxford, 1971, pp. 106–111. A contemporary use of the method with effervescent results is Norman O. Brown's *Love's Body,* Random House, 1966.

12. See George H. Williams, *op. cit.*

13. For an extraordinarily suggestive effort to link symbol, myth, and reflective thought see Paul Ricoeur, *The Symbolism of Evil,* Harper and Row, 1967. See also Mircea Eliade, *Images and Symbols,* Sheed and Ward, 1969; and my forthcoming *The Roots of Religious Consciousness.*

14. Perry Miller, *Nature's Nation,* Harvard University Press, 1967, p. 6.

15. *Winthrop Papers,* Vol. II, The Massachusetts Historical Society, 1931 pp. 294–295.

16. For a discussion of Winthrop's covenant theory see Perry Miller, *Errand into the Wilderness,* Harvard University Press, 1956, pp. 148–149.

17. There are many places in Augustine's writings where this contrast appears. One of the most central is *City of God,* XIV, 28.

18. Alan Heimert, *Religion and the American Mind,* Harvard University Press, 1966, p. 454.

19. *The Works of Jonathan Edwards*, Vol. II, Yale University Press, 1959.

20. Heimert, *op. cit.*, p. 459. On this interesting figure see William G. McLoughlin, *Isaac Backus and the American Pietistic Tradition*, Little, Brown, 1967.

21. Heimert, *op. cit.*, p. 458.

22. Quoted in Erik Erikson, *Dimensions of a New Identity* (Jefferson Lectures 1973), Norton, 1974, p. 89.

23. Jones, *op. cit.*, p. 238.

24. *Ibid.*, p. 254.

25. *Ibid.*, pp. 251–265.

26. Sellers, *op. cit.*, pp. 72–73.

27. Saul K. Padover (ed.), *The Complete Jefferson*, Duell, Sloan & Pearce, 1943, p. 414.

28. "If the image of God and the law of God were completely obliterated from man's soul by sin, if no 'faint outlines' of the original remained, men would have no conception of justice, righteousness, or peace to use as the foundation of the human standards of equity, fair-dealing, and order that are the pillars of civilized society. . . ." Herbert A. Deane, *The Political and Social Ideas of St. Augustine*, Columbia University Press, 1963, p. 96.

29. Heimert, *op. cit.*, p. 21.

30. *Ibid.*, p. 411.

31. *Ibid.*, p. 401.

32. Ruth Bloch in an unpublished paper, "Millennial Thought in the American Revolutionary Movement," 1973, has provided copious evidence for a connection I had only surmised.

33. In Conrad Cherry, *God's New Israel: Religious Interpretations of American Destiny*, Prentice-Hall, 1971, p. 67.

34. Arendt, *op. cit.*, p. 300.

35. Heimert, *op. cit.*, pp. 303–304.

36. *Ibid.*, pp. 518–519.

37. *Ibid.*, pp. 516–517.

38. *Ibid.*, p. 521.

39. Clinton Rossiter, *The Political Thought of the American Revolution*, Harvest Books, 1963, p. 200.

40. Gordon S. Wood, *The Creation of the American Republic, 1776–1787*, Norton, 1972, p. 612.

41. On Adams see Wood, *op. cit.*, chapter 14, and Paul K. Conkin, *Puritans and Pragmatists*, Dodd, Mead, 1968, chapter 4.

42. A long, reflective, and in my opinion profound essay on the basic tension in American culture that was published too recently to be taken fully into account in this book is Wilson Carey McWilliams, *The Idea of Fraternity in America*, University of California Press, 1973.

43. Arendt, *op. cit.*, p. 204.

44. Heimert, *op. cit.*, p. 15.

45. Erikson comments on Jefferson's words, "God forbid that we should ever be twenty years without . . . a rebellion," as follows: "Why twenty years? Did he, maybe, refer not only to history but also to the life cycle: God forbid anybody should be twenty years old without having rebelled?" *Op. cit.*, p. 72.

46. Arendt, *op. cit.*, p. 235.

47. Heimert, *op. cit.*, p. 548.

II   AMERICA AS A CHOSEN PEOPLE

1. Cherry, *op. cit.*, p. 116.

2. Ernest Lee Tuveson, *Redeemer Nation*, University of Chicago Press, 1968, pp. 156–157.

3. Cherry, *op. cit.*, pp. 224–225.

4. *Ibid.*, p. 227.

5. *Ibid.*, p. 228.

6. *Ibid.*, p. 26.

7. Williams, *op. cit.*, p. 107.

8. *Ibid.*, p. 102.

9. Perry Miller, *The New England Mind: From Colony to Province*, Harvard University Press, 1953, chapter 2.

10. Increase Mather, *An Earnest Exhortation to the Inhabitants of New-England*, Boston, 1776, p. 4, as quoted in Anne Kusener Nelson, "King Philip's War and the Hubbard-Mather Rivalry," *The William and Mary Quarterly*, 3rd Series, Vol. 27, No. 4, 1970, p. 624. This quotation is concrete evidence for what is implied in a recent *New Yorker* cartoon. Two pilgrims are depicted on board ship, one saying to the other, "Religious freedom is my immediate goal, but my long-range plan is to go into real estate."

11. Winthrop D. Jordan, *White over Black*, University of North Carolina Press, 1968, p. 299.

12. *Ibid.*, pp. 300–301.

13. What is from one point of view "private," in that it is not official and does not speak for the state, is from another point of view "public," in that it represents not the tradition of particular persons or groups in isolation from the general society but applies those particular traditions to the problems of the whole society. In this context we can understand how many Church leaders engaged in what Martin Marty has called "public theology." They spoke genuinely out of their own religious traditions but to the problems of the society as a whole.

14. Perry Miller, *The Life of the Mind in America*, Harcourt, Brace and World, 1965. William G. McLoughlin, *The American Evangelicals 1800–1900*, Harper Torchbooks, 1968, p. 26.

15. Miller, *Life of the Mind*, p. 11.

16. *Ibid.*, p. 71.

17. Alexis de Tocqueville, *Democracy in America*, Vintage Books, 1954, Vol. I, 436.

18. Staughton Lynd, *Intellectual Origins of American Radicalism*, Vintage, 1968. p. 132.

19. Seymour Martin Lipset, *The First New Nation*, Basic Books, 1963, p. 34.

20. Gilbert Hobbs Barnes, *The Anti-Slavery Impulse 1830–1849*, Harbinger, 1964, p. 79.

21. *Ibid.*, p. 82.

22. Sidney E. Mead, *The Lively Experiment*, Harper and Row, 1963, p. 73.

23. Conrad Cherry has pointed out to me that it was precisely in the Civil War poetry of Melville and Whitman that American poetry reached a new level of maturity.

24. Winthrop S. Hudson (ed.), *Nationalism and Religion in America*, Harper and Row, 1970, pp. 115–116.

25. Henry David Thoreau, *Walden and Civil Disobedience*, Signet, New American Library, 1960, p. 225.

26. Herman Melville, *Clarel*, Hendricks House, 1960, pp. 434, 481–483.

27. Hudson, *op. cit.*, p. 122.

28. F. O. Matthiessen (ed.), *Oxford Book of American Verse*, Oxford, 1950, p. 462.

29. Ralph Henry Gabriel, *The Course of American Democratic Thought*, The Ronald Press, 1956, p. 385.

III SALVATION AND SUCCESS IN AMERICA

1. Erik H. Erikson, *Childhood and Society*, Norton, 1963, p. 285.

2. Howard Mumford Jones, *The Pursuit of Happiness*, Cornell University Press, 1966, p. 1.

3. Moses Rischin (ed.), *The American Gospel of Success*, Quadrangle Books, 1965, p. 29.

4. Middlekauff, *op. cit.*, p. 202.

5. *Ibid.*, p. 257.

6. *Ibid.*, p. 271.

7. *Ibid.*, p. 272.

8. *Ibid.*, pp. 255, 257.

9. Charles L. Sanford, *The Quest for Paradise*, University of Illinois Press, 1961, p. 125.

10. D. H. Lawrence, *Studies in Classic American Literature*, Doubleday Anchor, 1953, p. 31.

11. Conrad Cherry suggests that I have overlooked Horace Bush-

nell (1802–1876) as a major 19th-century theologian worthy to rank with Edwards and the Niebuhrs. Also on Bushnell see the interesting comments of Philip Rieff in the Preface to his *On Intellectuals*, Doubleday Anchor, 1970, pp. ix–x.

12. Irvin G. Wyllie, *The Self-Made Man in America*, Free Press, 1966, p. 4.

13. Miller, *The Life of the Mind*, p. 53.

14. McLoughlin, *The American Evangelicals*, p. 208.

15. Wyllie, *op. cit.*, p. 61.

16. Gabriel, *op. cit.*, p. 157.

17. *Ibid.*, p. 158.

18. Quoted in K. Shapiro, Introduction, in Henry Miller, *Tropic of Cancer*, Grove Press, 1961, p. viii.

19. James Baldwin, *Nobody Knows My Name*, Dell, 1963, pp. 111–112.

20. Erikson, *Childhood and Society*, p. 308.

21. *Ibid.*, p. 319.

22. For some wise comments on this problem see Erikson, *Dimensions of a New Identity*, pp. 113–119.

IV NATIVISM AND CULTURAL PLURALISM IN AMERICA

1. Jordan, *op. cit.*, pp. 12–13.

2. Hudson, *op. cit.*, p. 92.

3. Hans Kohn, *American Nationalism*, Collier Books, 1961, p. 144.

4. *Ibid.*, p. 143.

5. *Ibid.*, pp. 143–144.

6. Milton M. Gordon, *Assimilation in American Life*, Oxford University Press, 1964, pp. 104–114.

7. Kohn, *op. cit.*, p. 145.

8. Gordon, *op. cit.*, p. 113.

9. Malcolm X, *Autobiography*, Grove Press, 1966, p. 136.

10. Harold Cruse, *The Crisis of the Negro Intellectual*, William Morrow, 1967, p. 456.

11. W. E. B. Du Bois, *The Souls of Black Folk*, Signet, 1959, p. 52. (Originally published in 1903.)

12. Gordon, *op. cit.*, pp. 224–232.

13. Horace M. Kallen, *Culture and Democracy in the United States*, Boni and Liveright, 1924.

14. Middlekauff, *op. cit.*, p. 92.

15. Lawrence, *op. cit.*, p. 73.

16. The use of the phrase "by any means necessary" by black activists shows how American they are.

17. William Greenbaum points out in "America in Search of a New

Ideal: An Essay on the Rise of Pluralism," Harvard Educational Review, Vol. 44, No. 3, 1974, that the fuel for the melting pot was not only *hope* but also *shame*, and that was indeed inflicted on the immigrants by the majority population.

18. Oscar Handlin, *The Uprooted*, Grosset and Dunlap, 1951, p. 304.

19. Du Bois, *op. cit.*, p. 52.

20. Eldridge Cleaver, *Soul on Ice*, Delta, 1968, p. 186.

21. Michael Novak, *The Rise of the Unmeltable Ethnics*, Macmillan, 1973.

22. Greenbaum, *op. cit.*

23. Isaac Berkson, *Theories of Americanization: A Critical Study with Special Reference to the Jewish Group*, Teachers College, Columbia University, p. 121.

24. *Ibid.*, p. 130.

25. R. W. B. Lewis, *The Trials of the Word*, Yale University Press, 1965, p. ix.

26. Newton Arvin, *Whitman*, Macmillan, 1938, p. 287.

V THE AMERICAN TABOO ON SOCIALISM

1. A new and very useful symposium on the weakness of American socialism has recently been published: John H. M. Laslett and Seymour Martin Lipset, *Failure of a Dream? Essays in the History of American Socialism*, Doubleday Anchor, 1974. In spite of the richness of this collection of previously published and new materials, the religious and cultural aspects of the problem are treated quite tangentially.

2. Yehoshua Arieli traces the origin of the terms "individualism" and "socialism" to the Saint-Simonians in early 19th-century France. He writes, "The term 'individualism' was coined by the Saint-Simonians to characterize the condition of men in nineteenth-century society—their uprootedness, their lack of ideals and common beliefs, their fragmentation, and their ruthless competitive and exploitative attitudes which evolved from this legitimized anarchy." *Individualism and Nationalism in American Ideology*, Penguin Books, 1966, p. 207. "Socialism" was a contrast term to "individualism" understood in that sense. See Chapter 10 of Arieli's book entitled *Individualism and Socialism: The Birth of Two New Concepts*.

3. Arieli, *op. cit.*, p. 273.

4. *Ibid.*, p. 332.

5. *The Complete Jefferson*, op. cit., pp. 678–679.

6. Arieli, *op. cit.*, p. 236.

7. Arthur M. Schlesinger, Jr., *Orestes A. Brownson*, Little, Brown, 1939, p. 90.

8. *Ibid.*, p. 91.

9. *Ibid.*, p. 92.

10. *Ibid.*, p. 67.

11. Arvin, *op. cit.*, p. 103.

12. *Ibid.*, p. 102.

13. *Ibid.*, p. 143.

14. Albert Fried, *Socialism in America*, Anchor, 1970, p. 265.

15. F. O. Matthiessen (ed.), *The James Family*, Knopf, 1948, p. 53.

16. *Ibid.*, pp. 60, 61, 63, 66.

17. Gabriel, *op. cit.*, p. 257.

18. Fried, *op. cit.*, p. 9.

19. Gabriel, *op. cit.*, p. 358.

20. Jean Y. Tussey (ed.), *Eugene Debs Speaks*, Pathfinder Press, 1970, p. 144.

21. *Ibid.*, p. 264.

22. *Ibid.*, p. 22.

23. Nick Salvatore, who is writing a dissertation on Debs at Berkeley, has been helpful in my understanding of this and other aspects of Debs's career.

24. David M. Potter, *People of Plenty*, University of Chicago Press, 1954, pp. 176–177.

25. Ralph Waldo Emerson, *The Complete Essays and Other Writings*, Modern Library, 1940, p. 520.

VI THE BIRTH OF NEW AMERICAN MYTHS

1. *The Works of Walt Whitman*, Vol. II, Funk and Wagnalls, 1968, pp. 256–257.

2. Quoted in R. W. B. Lewis, *The Poetry of Hart Crane, A Critical Study*, Princeton University Press, 1967, p. 228.

3. If, as I believe, we are choking on our own progress, perhaps we can agree with Max Horkheimer that what we need "is no longer the acceleration of progress, but rather the jumping out of progress [*der Sprung aus dem Fortschritt heraus*]." Quoted in Martin Jay, *The Dialectical Imagination, A History of the Frankfurt School and the Institute of Social Research, 1923–1930*, Little, Brown, 1973, p. 157.

4. I did field work in a Mormon community in New Mexico in 1953 and at that time read a great deal about the history of Mormonism. Recently I had the opportunity to read an as yet unpublished book on the Mormons, *The Evolution of Mormonism*, by Mark Leone. My remarks are in part indebted to Professor Leone who was also kind enough to make some helpful suggestions on my first draft.

5. See Cleanth Brooks, *William Faulkner: The Yoknapatapha Country*, Yale University Press, 1963.

6. My account of the life and death of Larry Casuse is based on

Calvin Trillin, "U. S. Journal: Gallup, N. M." in *The New Yorker*, May 12, 1973.

7. *Ibid.*, p. 127.

8. *Ibid.*, p. 131.

9. Nathaniel Hawthorne, *The Marble Faun*, Chapter 18, Signet Edition, 1961, p. 122.

10. Melville, *Clarel*, p. 52.

11. *Ibid.*, pp. 483–484.

12. See Jonathan Edwards, *The Nature of True Virtue*, University of Michigan Press, 1960, and for Backus the passage on page 20 above.

13. See Robert N. Bellah, *Beyond Belief*, Part III. I do not mean to imply that the many serious problems involved in the reappropriation of traditional religious symbols in the present cultural situation have all been solved.

14. Much of this section is based on research on religious consciousness among young people in the San Francisco Bay area conducted by a research group under the direction of Charles Glock and myself between 1971 and 1974.

15. Robert N. Bellah, "No Direction Home—Religious Aspects of the American Crisis," in Myron B. Bloy, Jr., *Search for the Sacred: The New Spiritual Quest*, Seabury, 1972, p. 68.

16. Herman Melville, *Moby Dick*, chapter 23, Modern Library, 1950, p. 105.